Pr

In the writing of th aim to bring some light to the very serious subject of the 'Troubles' in Northern Ireland, in particular a certain time , 1986. As a Royal Marine serving with 45 commandos my experiences are written a rather narrow perspective, me being just a Marine on the ground, doing what I'm told to do. The stories or 'Dits' as we call them are all true accounts by me, recalled from memories 35 years after the events.

My research involved the use of the internet by searching for certain dates when events coincided with my own recollections, my stories have been told over many times during the years as I've travelled the world mixing with likeminded and experienced former military people with similar experiences.

The reflective process has helped me in my personal development with the aim of letting out emotions which have been pent up in the dark recesses of my mind for all these years. I have learned a lot more about the 'Troubles' through my research , more than I ever knew when I patrolled the streets of West Belfast or crawled through the field of South Armagh.

The book takes the reader on a personal journey when I join the Royal Marines at the age of 16 years old to when I left ten years later in 1989 the year when I started my now 30 years offshore as a Commercial Diver, Supervisor and eventually Diving Superintendent.

Enjoy the 'Dits'

Reflection 1979-1989

Contents

Like they say, every story has a beginning. Mine starts when I joined the Royal Marines who installed values and honesty. I'm proud to say that I still try to live my life according to those values. I have a strong sense of justice. It's pretty much black-and-white. I don't see too much grey as a pragmatist. I think it's important to protect family. I work hard offshore 6 months of the year. At the same time, I like to have quality time off and believe life's too short to dwell on the past or rest on your laurels.

Informal humour is perhaps surprisingly critical to the operation of commando units. There are other informal methods by which the ethos of the Royal Marines is maintained.

One of the most important of these is the telling of stories about events which have occurred to Royal Marines on or off operations. “Spinning dits" has become almost institutionalized among the Corps so that this story-telling has become a recognized form of socializing. It constitutes an important element of Royal Marines leisure time in in bars or even books like this one, which dits are told. The term “dit" seems to be derived from the naval term, „ditty-box". This was a box in which sailors kept personal items. However, the meaning seems to have changed somewhat by the mid-20th century. Contributors to the Globe and Laurel sent their reports from the „ditty box" The ditty-box here seems to refer to the desk at which correspondents wrote or to a box or bag in which he kept his own notes, from which the report would be compiled. It seems probable that the term “dit" then became specifically attached to the stories, stored in or sent from the „ditty-box".

‘The troubles’

The Troubles were an ethno-nationalist conflict in Northern Ireland during the late 20th century Known internationally, as the Northern Ireland conflict. The conflict began in the late 1960s and is usually deemed to have ended with the Good Friday Agreement of 1998. Although the Troubles primarily took place in Northern Ireland, at times the violence spilled over into parts of the Republic of Ireland, England, and mainland Europe. The conflict was primarily political and nationalistic, fuelled by historical events. It also had an ethnic or sectarian dimension, but despite the use of the terms "Protestant" and "Catholic" to refer to the two sides, it was not a religious conflict. A key issue was the constitutional status of Northern Ireland. Unionists, who were mostly Ulster Protestants, wanted Northern Ireland to remain within the United Kingdom. Irish nationalists, who were mostly Irish Catholics, wanted Northern Ireland to leave the United Kingdom and join a united Ireland. The conflict began during a campaign by the Northern Ireland Civil Rights Association to end discrimination against the Catholic/nationalist minority by the Protestant/unionist government of Northern Ireland and Royal Ulster Constabulary (RUC). The authorities attempted to suppress the protest campaign with police brutality; it was also met with violence from loyalists, who believed it was a republican front. Increasing tensions led to severe violence in August 1969 and the deployment of British troops, in what became the British Army's longest ever operation. 'Peace walls' were built in some areas to keep the two communities apart. Some Catholics initially welcomed the British Army as a more neutral force than the RUC, but it soon came to be seen as hostile and biased, particularly after Bloody Sunday in 1972. Armed paramilitary organisations joined the fray, quickly becoming the most violent actors in the conflict. The main participants in the Troubles were republican paramilitaries such as the Provisional Irish Republican Army (IRA) and the Irish National Liberation Army (INLA); loyalist paramilitaries such as the Ulster Volunteer Force (UVF) and Ulster Defence Association (UDA); British state security forces, the British Army and RUC; and political activists and politicians. The security forces of the Republic of Ireland played a smaller role. Republican paramilitaries carried out a guerrilla campaign against British security forces as well as a bombing campaign against infrastructural, commercial, and political targets. Loyalists targeted republicans/nationalists and attacked the wider Catholic community in what they described as retaliation. At times, there were bouts of sectarian tit-for-tat violence, as well as feuds within and between paramilitary groups of the same stripe. The British security forces undertook both a policing and counter-insurgency role, primarily against republicans. There were some incidents of collusion between British security forces and loyalist paramilitaries. The Troubles also involved numerous riots, mass protests and acts of civil disobedience, and led to increased segregation and the creation of no-go areas. More than 3,500 people were killed in the conflict, of which 52% were civilians, 32% were members of the British security forces and 16% were members of paramilitary groups. Republican paramilitaries were responsible for some 60% of the deaths, loyalists 30% and security forces 10%. There has been sporadic violence since the Good Friday Agreement was signed, including on-going punishment attacks and a campaign by dissident republicans.

My stories "Dits"

Just back from the Falklands war back in 1982, I had a drunken conversation with another Royal Marine standing at a bar in the small town of Poole, Dorset. He was a sergeant, PW1 Sniper who had served two tours of Northern Ireland as a '14 int' operative, as his story unfolded, he asked if I recognized the story. No, I said.

Harry's Game a novel by G. Seymour which involves the efforts, by British army captain Harry Brown, the hunter, to identify and bring to justice his 'game', the Provo assassin. The difficulties of planting an agent in the parts of Belfast controlled by the IRA are given in some detail as Harry is briefed for the task and it comes as no surprise to the reader, in fact, it seems almost inevitable, when one of these leads to suspicion of the stranger.

In the Belfast of those days even the slightest suspicion could have fatal consequences and an absorbing and compelling race against time is presented as Harry tries to identify his man before he's identified by the Provo's. The pace never slackens for a moment. Although Harry, perhaps more by luck than investigative skill is well on the way to locating his man, events occur that place him in danger. These are magnified after the brilliantly written scene with Josephine in the Sperrins, after which Harry realizes that affairs are fast approaching a climax. When that finally arrives it is surprising, exciting, and totally believable a fitting end to an absorbing story.

When this book was first published in 1978, however, the British army was very much involved in containing the threat posed by the 'Provo's'. It was the first time that the events in Northern Ireland had been the subject of a book of this kind. The thriller, of course, is regarded as an entertainment but there is truly little of that in this novel, Gerald Seymour's first. Instead, there is intolerance, suspicion, violence, and fear in abundance. Harry's Game grips, educates, perhaps, but never entertains in the light-hearted sense of that word.

Pete tells me that in his debrief with the commanding officer of his unit, a man sat in the corner of the CO's office taking notes on a small note pad. This man was Gerald Seymour in his reporting days in the 1970s He says Northern Ireland was one of the most challenging stories he ever covered as a journalist.

He admits that he tries to find people who will talk to him off the record and non-attributably, people on the fringes of the dirty raincoat brigade, well Pete tells the story, and the only difference in real life is, the ending of the book story where his mate dies and not him. A few days after the conversation while training for a display we both had to abseil 200 feet from a hovering helicopter. Pete nearly hung himself as he whipped in the rope to slow down his decent, the end of the rope whipped up and around his neck leaving him hanging ten feet from the deck. Luckily the dispatcher told the pilot, and the pilot lowered the chopper and Pete to the deck saving his life, lucky man.

The story about Harry's Game had me fixated and wanted to be involved with the secretive war being fought over the water in Northern Ireland, but it would take me a further 3 years before getting into the action as part of 45 commando's emergency tour of West Belfast, from the 2nd of July until the 10th of November 1986.

In Northern Ireland, people belonging to the two main religion/politico groups normally have relatively fixed stereotypes about one another. Catholics in Northern Ireland saw Protestants as power holders, bigoted, loyalist, and murderers. Protestants saw Catholics as priest-ridden, breeding like rabbits, superstitious. Both groups saw themselves as fine, decent people, but saw each other as bitter and brainwashed.

We can be a conscious or unconscious of discrimination. Even if one does not consciously discriminate, very often our membership of a ruling group can make us an unconscious agent of discrimination. Our behaviour can also be discriminatory in its effect, even though not in intention, as a young Marine I was ignorant of many facts regarding the situation in Northern Ireland as I was there to do my job. But prejudice is an opinion held in advance about something, someone or some group without good reason or adequate knowledge or experience. Prejudice is about feelings and beliefs, and it can influence our perception. There is a good deal of evidence to show that what we believe influences the way we see an event, people are not usually prejudiced because of what they see or hear but will see or hear people and events differently because of what we believe.

In 1986, 45 Commando Recce troop had been designated 'Close observation troop' to operate in the South Armagh area, while the rest of the unit were to be operating in the Belfast area as the Emergency 'Roulement Battalion'.

The Royal Marines conducted 40 Tours of Duty in Northern Ireland during Op Banner, as well as providing manpower for special intelligence operations they were also involved in long term operational commitments such as Operations Lifespan and Sealion.

Royal Marine units sent to Northern Ireland after 1978 had a professional attitude and commitment to be the best. The units involved with counterintelligence operations especially after the Murder of the Colonel Commandant of the Royal

Marines, Admiral of the Fleet, and The Earl Mountbatten of Burma by the IRA. Mountbatten usually holidayed at his summer home, Classiebawn Castle, in Mullaghmore, a small seaside village in County Sligo.

The village was only 12 miles from the border with Northern Ireland and near an area known to be used as a cross-border refuge by IRA members. In 1978, the IRA had allegedly attempted to shoot Mountbatten as he was aboard his boat, but poor weather had prevented the sniper taking his shot.

On 27 August 1979, Mountbatten went lobster-potting and tuna fishing in his 30-foot wooden boat, Shadow V, which had been moored in the harbour at Mullaghmore. IRA member Thomas McMahon had slipped onto the unguarded boat that night and attached a radio-controlled bomb weighing 50 pounds. When Mountbatten was aboard, just a few hundred yards from the shore, the bomb was detonated. The boat was destroyed by the force of the blast, and Mountbatten's legs were almost blown off. Mountbatten, then aged 79, was pulled alive from the water by nearby fishermen, but died from his injuries before being brought to shore.

Also aboard the boat were his elder daughter Patricia, her husband John, their twin sons Nicholas and Timothy Knatchbull, John's mother Doreen, Lady Brabourne, and Paul Maxwell, a young crew member from County Fermanagh. Nicholas (aged 14) and Paul (aged 15) were killed by the blast and the others were seriously injured. Doreen, Lady Brabourne (aged 83) died from her injuries the following day.

The IRA issued a statement afterward, saying: The IRA claim responsibility for the execution of Lord Louis Mountbatten. This operation is one of the discriminate ways we can bring to the attention of the English people the continuing occupation of our country. The death of Mountbatten and the tributes paid to him will be seen in sharp contrast to the apathy of the British Government and the English people to the deaths of over three hundred British soldiers, and the deaths of Irish men, women, and children at the hands of their forces. The IRA claimed responsibility for the bombing, calling it an "execution," and also took responsibility for two roadside bombs that went off the same day 18 hours later. The roadside bombs killed 18 British troops and one civilian in Northern Ireland, later known as the Warrenpoint ambush. The IRA exploded the remote-control bombs from a firing point on the other side of the river, in the Republic of Ireland.

Six soldiers travelling in an Army vehicle were killed by the first bomb and as colleagues arrived to help, a second device detonated, killing 12 more troops.

Warrenpoint or the Narrow Water bombings were pivotal in Irish-British relations as the event which instigated the British policy of "Ulsterisation", whereupon the RUC would be given more powers to deal "in house" with the security threat. The purpose of this was so that the British public would stop asking of their government sticky questions such as "why are we in the North of Ireland in the first place?" and so the problem could be passed back to the North and effectively to the island of Ireland, becoming well and truly "the Irish problem".

Then In 1981 Lieutenant-General Sir Stewart Pringle who at the time was the Commandant-General of the Royal Marines survived an IRA bomb attack of the type that killed Airey Neave MP. The device exploded in his car shortly after he drove away from his south

London home. Knowing the capacity of the IRA for secondary devices, his immediate action was to warn would-be rescuers to stand clear of the scene.

He was lucky to be alive. The story famously goes that he was headed out for a run with his dog, Bella, and, on regaining his composure, asked his rescuer bravely, "How is my dog?". Seriously injured he lost his right leg below the knee, Sir Stewart displayed the courage that personified him by carrying on serving the corps.

When NP8901 returned defeated from the Falklands, not knowing what the type of reception awaiting us as we landed at RAF Brize Norton in Oxfordshire, about 75 mi west north-west of London, the largest station of the Royal Air Force. It is close to the villages of Brize Norton on the 6th of April 1982 we all gathered inside an aircraft hangar waiting for an address from the Commandant-General of the Royal Marines, Lieutenant-General Sir Stewart Pringle.

An attaché brought Sir Stewart Pringle out into the airport hangar in his wheelchair, where he prepared to deliver an address. All the lads in NP8901 stood in awe of the wounded hero, but when the moment came for our greeting, Pringle did us an unexpected turn. The dignified man stood up and moved out of his wheelchair and beamed out upon us.

Pringle wanted to personally shake each of our hands. Looking him in the eye, taking his still rugged grip in mine, was one of the proudest moments of my life. For that moment, the deafening roar washed away, and it was only the two of us.

When we finally settled in to listen to his speech, Stewart Pringle spoke in a voice both clear and true. Then the wounded man performed what felt like his second miraculous turn as Commandant General on that day.

He told all of us that we would be going back. As that truth sank in, each one of us was filled with a pride we had never experienced before. We would be a vital part of a task force that, as we soon learned, was already in the process of mobilizing in the South Atlantic.

Our moment of infamy would soon be redeemed. We would take back the Falkland Islands; our part would be the attack on Mount Harriet 11-12th of June 1982, having joined 42 commandos as 'J' Company.

Sir Stewart Pringle achieved all this at a time when the very existence of the then 317-year-old Royal Marines was in doubt, following a review by John Nott, the then Secretary of State for Defence. The terrible injuries created a truce in his personal battle to save the Marines, but when Argentina invaded the Falklands, it was to Pringle's Marines that the Ministry of Defence turned, and the conflict effectively saved the Corps. As Commanding Officer of 45 Commando in two tours of Northern Ireland he was a well-respected man and once again the Marines deployed to Northern Ireland wanted to prove their worth by being professional and productive during the tours on active service.

The Unit 45 Commando had a good record during the troubles only losing 4 men over 4 tours: Cpl D Leach, murdered by PIRA, 13/08/1974; Mne M Southern, murdered by PIRA, 13/08/1974; Mne N Bewley, murdered by PIRA, 12/08/1977; Sgt W Corbett, Shot Accidentally, 23/08/1981.

The year 1986 had not started well when in January Two Royal Ulster Constabulary officers were killed while on foot patrol in Thomas Street in Armagh. The Irish Republican Army exploded a remote-controlled bomb that had been hidden in a litter bin. Then in February an off-duty RUC officer and a Catholic civilian were killed in an Irish Republican Army gun attack on the Talk of the Town bar in Maguiresbridge, County Fermanagh.

In March It was announced that additional British Army soldiers would be sent to Northern Ireland to support the Royal Ulster Constabulary. Later, in the month The Royal Ulster Constabulary announced a ban on a planned Apprentice Boys of Derry march in Portadown, County Armagh. The decision sparked serious rioting between Loyalists and the police that was to continue off and on over the following weeks. Loyalist gangs carried out petrol bomb attacks on 11 Catholic homes in Lisburn, County Antrim. RUC officers were also the subject of intimidation from Loyalists.

On April the first there were further periods of rioting in Portadown, County Armagh. During the riots Keith White, a Protestant civilian, was fatally wounded by a plastic baton round fired by the Royal Ulster Constabulary. White died on 14 April 1986 and was the first Protestant to be killed by a plastic bullet. Police figures released later showed that there were: 38 civilians injured; 39 RUC officers injured; 147 plastic baton rounds fired; 38 cases of damage to property; and 33 arrests.

May 1986, Two Royal Ulster Constabulary officers and one British soldier were killed by the Irish Republican Army near Crossmaglen, County Armagh. The three men had been part of a joint RUC, British Army foot patrol when the IRA detonated a remote-controlled bomb hidden in a ditch by the side of the road. IEDs are the terrorists' weapon of choice because they require limited skills to build and provide dramatic results for little investment of time, money, and effort. The public relations benefit of a surprising spectacular explosion far outweighs that resulting from attacks using more conventional weapons. Given terrorists' easy access to commercial technologies, training, and the ability to either make or obtain explosive materials, IEDs continue to provide the enemy inexpensive, stand-off, precision weapons systems with near-total anonymity. IEDs are the greatest casualty producer in 21st century warfare and a long-standing threat to security forces and civilian populations. We needed technologies to improve the speed of inspection of culverts and surveillance of nefarious activity, around the vicinity. This has been motivated by lessons learned in the south and a desire for readily available technology to mitigate the effectiveness of culverts as a location for improvised explosive device (IED) emplacement. We needed innovative solutions for surveillance and inspection in or around roadway culverts, tunnels under roadways, and roadway craters to defeat IED emplacements. This technology had not yet been found or utilized during the 80's as the IRA used the culvert IED's to great effect

June 24th Ian Paisley, then leader of the Democratic Unionist Party, said that "Northern Ireland was on the verge of civil war" Why? Because if you take away the forums of democracy you don't have anything left. He said this after been forcibly carried out from the Assembly building by police in 1986. The Democratic Unionist Party is a unionist and loyalist political party in Northern Ireland. It was founded in 1971 during the Troubles by Ian Paisley, who led the party for the next 37 years.

July 2nd, we arrived in Armagh City to witness the annual Orange Order parades, where violence flared when Orangemen converged on the town in the evening after their annual marches to commemorate the Battle of the Boyne. A group of Protestant youths started throwing missiles at the police, as they attempted to section off Catholic areas. Disturbances continued into the night with nationalist and loyalist rioters directing their anger against the security forces and each other.

Vehicles overturned and the police attacked with darts, bottles and stones. Four were seriously injured including one who was dragged from his car and stabbed in the neck in Portadown, the march to Drumcree Church had been permitted by the Royal Ulster Constabulary that year to pass through the mainly Catholic Obins Street area of the town. The RUC also announced that the 'Twelfth' parade would be re-routed from Obins Street. There was rioting in the town when the RUC prevented George Seawright, a Loyalist councillor, and other non-local Orangemen from entering the Catholic area.

On the 9th Two British soldiers were killed by a remote-controlled bomb while they were on foot patrol near Crossmaglen, County Armagh. The attack was carried out by the Irish Republican Army.

We had arrived during interesting times, much of it down to the Anglo-Irish Agreement signed in 1985 by the Irish prime minister Garret FitzGerald and for the British government Margaret Thatcher on Friday 15 November 1985 the Anglo-Irish Agreement was Signed by Margaret Thatcher, then British Prime Minister, and Garret FitzGerald, then Taoiseach (Irish Prime Minister), at Hillsborough,

County Down, on behalf of the two governments. The first part of the document stated: "The two Governments (a) affirm that any change in the status of Northern Ireland would only come about with the consent of a majority of the people of Northern Ireland." The Agreement established the Inter-Governmental Conference that for the first time gave the Irish government a consultative role in matters related to security, legal affairs, politics, and cross-border co-operation. The Agreement also stated that the two governments would support any future wish by the people of Northern Ireland to enter into a united Ireland. Many Nationalists saw this as an important development. Unionists were outraged at the Agreement and began a long campaign to have the AIA removed. The AIA was only superseded when the Good Friday Agreement was implemented on 2 December 1999.

Loyalist paramilitaries also reacted, and the Ulster Freedom Fighters (UFF) declared all members of the Anglo-Irish Conference and Secretariat to be 'legitimate targets'. Ian Gow, then British Treasury Minister, resigned in protest at the signing of the Agreement.

While not disregarding the contemporary important emphasis on issues of race and ethnicity emerging, they face in Ireland a different but equally destructive manifestation of discrimination. The daily challenge comes from living and working in a community deeply divided by religious difference. Daily they must face the seemingly endless litany of loss, death, destruction, and bitterness caused by those from both sides of the community who are prepared to resort to violence as a means of achieving their political ends.

The pervasive values of the paramilitaries are inimical to society. Yet the problems of division and discrimination, either as victim or perpetrator, are not monopolized by the men and women of violence. Everyone becomes contaminated in direct or indirect, in overt or subtle ways. None who live in Ulster are immune from either the causes or the consequences of discrimination which provide a seedbed in which violence flourishes. No one is allowed to be neutral.

If they are not already labeled by birth as belonging to one side or the other, "prod" or "taig", they are quickly assigned by family, friends. within the context of a deeply divided society in which it has become almost commonplace for small minorities to pursue their ends by actively planning and perpetrating violence which appears to be condoned to some extent by some sections of the population who have grown passive either through intimidation, threat or fear of threat, indifference, or weariness.

So my story started before a few years before the 1986 deployment to Northern Ireland, in fact starting back in 1979 the year I joined the Royal Marines at the age of sixteen and a half years old.

The Royal Marines were first formed in 1664 as sea-soldiers for the Second Dutch War. The long history of the Corps is a source of pride to serving marines and the Globe and Laurel, the Corps cap-badge. They encompass the three components of the fighting power the Physical assets and the moral values of the men. Their ethos refers simply to how the Marines actually fight and how they organize and prepare to do so. Ethos is the mission and the means. However, the claim often made by Royal Marines that their ethos is sacred and is magical, despite occasionally misperceptions, fully recognize that ethos refers to what we do and how we do it. Often cited by marines, when discussing ethos is the following poem 'The Law for the Wolves', by Rudyard Kipling.

'For the strength of the pack is the wolf, and the strength of the wolf is the pack.'

For the Royal Marines to be a unified group members of the Corps must invest their relationship with each other with a special power; they regard themselves as obligated to each other. The ethos refers to the common goals which the Royal Marines pursue and how they achieve them.

The Royal Marines are the guardian of the commando standards, determining who will be allowed to join this exclusive club. The Royal Marines undergo the longest basic training of any Infantry force in the world, 32 weeks, at the Commando Training Centre Royal Marines, Lympstone in Devon. The Royal Marines are the only part of the British Armed Forces where Officers and Other Ranks are trained at the same location. Much of the basic training is carried out on the rugged terrain of Dartmoor and Woodbury common with a significant proportion taking place at night.

The first weeks of training are spent learning basic skills that will be used later. The washing behind your foreskin demonstration during the hygiene lecture always amuses, looking back on that observation as one of the training team stood naked in the shower pulling back his foreskin too gently! Wash his penis with the water while having a shower. A second member of the training team giving the a blow by blow account of the operation using his best lecture voice, saying “If you have a foreskin, pull it back gently and wash underneath. If you don't wash underneath the foreskin correctly, a cheesy-looking substance called smegma may begin to gather. Smegma is a natural lubricant that keeps the penis moist. It's found on the head of the penis and under the foreskin as presented by Corporal Kennedy in front of you” this then followed by a warning.

“If smegma builds up in the foreskin, it can start to smell, stop you easily pulling your foreskin back, and become a breeding ground for bacteria. This can cause redness and swelling of the head of your penis, called balanitis” we had been warned. This lecture the will be etched into the young minds of all recruits for a lifetime. During the early weeks, time is spent on the parade ground and on the rifle ranges. Physical training at this stage emphasizes all-round body strength, to develop the muscles necessary to carry the heavy weights a marine will use in an operational unit. Key milestones include a gym pass-out at week 9, which shows that a recruit is ready for the Bottom Field, a battle swimming test, and learning to do a "regain" every recruits nightmare for various reasons, the aim is to hang under the rope fully kitted then climb back onto the horizontal rope running across a water tank without falling in! a necessity. Most of these tests are completed with the ever present "fighting order" of 32 lb. of equipment. Individual field craft skills are also taught at this basic stage.

Week 10 and we moved into the exercise called Hunters Moon

Monday morning, everyone is packed and rearing to go for the toughest exercise in in early training. We did day navigation all the way to our location following our route card in which then finally led us to the Training Teams home for the first few days. On the night we had a night navigation exercise which was our first one as a section with no Corporal to help or guide us if we messed up. We had to fully prepare our route cards and get all our bearings as accurate as we could so we didn't get lost on our first night.

The next day Tuesday, we did our day navigation followed by a stalk on Dartmoor which majority of us passed and then we yomped to a different location to do re-sections, and a static map reading test. Then as usual for the night we did sentry duty all night till morning ready for the "BIG YOMP"

Wednesday, we all got up early feeling nervous for the "nod killer yomp" which was 9km to Princetown which took 1 hour and 30 minutes but after the first 10 minutes it was clearly to say the whole troop was finding the task difficult ! But we cracked on. We started the second half of the yomp which was 12km to the location, on the way there we went the “roller coaster” route which was steep hills and boggy areas, all hanging out but managed to stay closed up and cracked on, we finally got to our location mentally and physically fatigued, however, we did it. On that night the training team stripped us of our weapons and equipment so we had nothing but a knife and our survival tin.

Thursday, we built shelters using material around us like sticks, logs and moss, the natural environment, we collected firewood and set up traps and wires for fishing, the ML’s (mountain leaders) came down and teach us how to gut a fish properly by taking the bones out and how to kill a chicken humanely for food during the day and collect local food supplies such as berries to keep going and water from the stream to boil it for 15 mins so it was sterile enough to drink. We had to do this for 24 hours, just surviving off the environment .

Friday, we survived knowing we had reached the end of the toughest exercise in this phase of training. There was a three kilometre extraction yomp, to our final destination where we got picked up and transported back to camp. finally all made it and not a single person failed the exercise, this gave us massive morale boost as we made it as a troop and not individuals this was the first time we bonded a troop by the end of the famous, Hunter Moon.

The week 24

With only two weeks to go until we enter the Commando Phase of training, 252 Troop had a run through session of the Endurance Course and a taster of the Tarzan Assault Course. It was an eye opener of the level we had to reach to pass out and become a Royal Marine Commandos.

The majority of the week was spent learning the basic drills of the GPMG, skills such as the load and unload drill, normal safety procedures, this done to ensure that the weapon has not rounds in the chamber and is safe, Barrel Changes and the immediate actions if a problem occurs with the gun. These skills would then be used for the live fire shoot at the end of the wee. We all took part on the live shoot on the Saturday morning at Straight Point and all successfully passed.

The Friday morning was the big test of the week, the 12 mile load carry. Similar to the run at the start of the week it wasn't the hardest test we had done at CTC but we could feel it in our legs by the end.

Week 25 commenced with an early afternoon trip to our first experience of HMS Raleigh. The troop had been looking forward to this week finally getting to learn another key skill of a Royal Marine….amphibious assault!

As much as we wanted to get to grips with the landing craft first we had to learn some of the basics about being on board a ship, this started with fire fighting. The next day was learning about sea survival. Again more classroom time was in order to familiarize ourselves with the life rafts and all the equipment. Practical evolutions followed starting with trying to get the full survival suit on against the clock which was not ideal to do but definitely funny to watch! Then we had a fair amount of time in the pool working as a team with the staff there giving us various survival scenarios.

Next we would meet the LC rating which started with a dip in the ice cold water to learn how to how to right a capsized zodiac, ideal start to the day! We then had talks on each of the boats, before jumping on the landing craft vehicle personnel (LCVP) to get to our next location. En route we practiced transitioning from boat to boat which was fun but wet. We also had a go at landing on a beach from various vessels. Once we arrived at our location we waited for night to fall in a hangar which was a nice rest. We then practiced landing on a beach at night from a zodiac deployed from an LCVP which was enjoyable. Overall it was a great week which we learnt a lot of new skills which we will be using when were on the final exercise next week.

Week 26 was quite a rushed week for 252 troops we only had five days to complete exercise which is the final confirmatory exercise that we have to complete in order to proceed towards the final weeks of commando training.

The whole exercise was mentally and physically demanding however extremely enjoyable. Throughout the gruelling days we performed a variety of operations and tasks. Such as Recce patrols where we would find info on the enemy we were dealing with, such as size location and disposition. Other operations we performed were a precise set ambush which was tedious but exhilarating at the same time, as we were waiting there for a good seven hours over night till morning. Once the ambush was over we then gathered info that the enemy was moving south.

Another task we did with the LC's (landing craftsmen) who are in control of all the amphibious vehicles such as the Zodiacs, Orcs (Offshore Raiding Craft), etc. We had orders from the Troop commander to dominate a position and destroy any threats that were on top of a cliff, which meant at night we boarded the zodiacs and went across to the rocks near the cliff face. There is a lot of yomping to do, In other words we covered the whole of Dartmoor!

The culmination of this training is a period known as the Commando Course. Since the creation of the British Commandos during World War II, all Royal Marines complete the Commando course as part of their training. Key aspects of the course include climbing and rope work techniques, patrolling, and amphibious operations. This intense phase ends with a series of tests which have remained virtually unchanged since World War II. Again, these tests, and indeed virtually all the training, are done with a "fighting order “on.

The commando tests are taken on consecutive days, they include a nine-mile speed march, carrying full fighting order, to be completed in 90 minutes. The Endurance course is a six-mile, course across rough terrain at Woodbury Common near Lympstone, which includes tunnels, pipes, wading pools, and an underwater culvert. The course ends with a four-mile run back to the camp followed by a marksmanship test to be completed in 72 minutes. The Course ends at the 25m range where we must then put at least 6 out of 10 shots on target without cleaning our weapon.

The Tarzan Assault, Course. This is an assault course combined with an aerial confidence test. It starts with a death slide and ends with a rope climb up a thirty-foot vertical wall. It must be completed with full fighting order in 13 minutes.

The Thirty milers: This is a 30-mile march across Dartmoor, wearing fighting order, and additional safety equipment. It must be completed in 8 hours, who must also navigate the route themselves, rather than following a DS with the rest of a syndicate and carry their own equipment. The day after the 30-mile march, any who failed any of the tests may attempt to retake them.

As one of the original twelve out of sixty five boys who joined 252 troop which passed all the tests and gained the converted Green Beret I was still not old enough to be deployed to active service in Northern Ireland, as still under the age of seventeen and a half years old, we needed more experience in a commando unit. My first unit being 40 Commando who at the time were based in Seaton barracks, crown hill Plymouth. Completing the Commando Course successfully entitles the recruit or officer to wear the coveted Green Beret but does not mean that the Royal Marine has finished his training. That decision will be made by the troop or batch training team and will depend on the recruit's or young officer's overall performance.

After basic and commando training, a Royal Marine Commando will normally join a unit of 3 Commando Brigade. At the time there was three Royal Marines Commando infantry units in the Brigade: 40 Commando located in Plymouth, 42 Commando at Bickleigh Barracks, near Plymouth, and 45 Commando at HMS Condor, Arbroath on the east coast of Scotland.

Royal Marines may then go on to undertake specialist training in a variety of skills, Platoon Weapons Instructor, Mortar operator, signals, clerks, sniper, PT instructor, Mountain

Leader, Swimmer Canoeist, chef, Landing Craft coxswain.

Training for these specializations may be undertaken at CTCRM or in a joint environment, my technical training as Heavy weapons HW3, Milan, anti-tank operator course done in-house at Seaton barracks. MILAN uses a Semi-Automatic Command Line of Sight (SACLOS) guidance system with a thin wire used to transmit guidance information from the firing post to the missile. A Milan is an anti-tank weapon, which fires a guided missile with a very substantial warhead over a range of 2,000 meters.

Having completed the course it was my choice not to join support company but join B company as the sprog GPMG carrier, as all Marines will tell you, the youngest to join the section will always be pinged as the gunner because weighing in at nearly 14kg no one wanted to carry the thing, everyone wanted to fire the thing especially in a contact. As the 4-troop gunner, August 1980 I took part in the exercise Teamwork, a summer Norway, beach landing from HMS Bulwark the year just before its decommissioning later that year.

Desperate to see action I scanned daily orders looking for opportunities, one came up for a detachment on board a vessel operating in the waters of Northern Ireland which if served on would qualify for a campaign medal, but I never got the draft.

Putting in for a draft was simple you just asked, if picked you were off, I put in for draft to Naval Party 8901, NP8901 and my request was accepted so left 40 Commando after nearly two years to join my new unit in Poole Dorset in 1982 destined for the Falklands islands. I asked someone where the Falkland Island was located in the world and he replied “off Scotland” and walked away laughing.

A stretch on the South Atlantic seemed as good as any to spend a year of my time. It was a secluded place, far away from any distractions.

As my new mates and I prepared for our transfer, none of us knew about international tensions, regarding the islands. No one knew what was brewing between our government and the Argentineans. None of us knew a thing about crumbled talks at the United Nations, and none of us really had to. As the date for our departure crept ever nearer, all any one of us saw as challenging was the prospect of spending a year sequestered with the ugly mug next to us as company.

From the first moment I arrived, the Falkland Islands felt very small. The Marine barracks up in Moody Brook were dingy and hardly inviting. Brown carpet. Wooden walls. The bar was closed, but the smell of beer reeked from the stained furniture.

I wondered what I was getting myself into coming down here, for a year no less. No matter how I looked at this place, it hardly felt inviting.

We had been brought to the Falkland Islands urgently, but so far, we had not been told a single thing about why. I kept thinking that all of us were being treated like mushrooms - kept in the dark and fed shit. As Marines, we may be accustomed to operating on a need-to-know basis, but the constant feeling of not knowing took a gradual toll on us. Most of us usually coped with the stresses of military life by blowing off with a few pints and throwing around a lot of tough talk, but the bar near the barracks appeared as though it never opened for business.

With no other word on what was to come next, I fell back on my goals.

There would be my training, and I was determined to get into good shape.

The Falklands War provided the backdrop to the next action of the Royal Marines. Argentina invaded the islands in April 1982.

Our assignment was supposed to be peaceful. We were part of a simple rotation, coming in as the replacement detachment for the lads that had been stationed down there for the months before us. By late in March, though, we had all been made aware that at least some fighting was imminent. There was tension in the air. Aggressive overtures by the Argentine army revealed that they stood on the brink of invasion, ready to take back the islands that they thought were rightfully theirs. It was around 3 P.M. local time, on the previous day, when the other shoe finally dropped on us. It was on a Thursday, April the first when Rex Hunt, British Governor of the Falkland

Islands, received an ominous telex from Military Intelligence.

We have apparently reliable evidence that an Argentine task force will gather off Cape Pembroke early tomorrow morning, 2nd April. You will wish to make your dispositions accordingly.

Our detachment sorted out the news while kicking around in the bar within our barracks. As I remember, the boys from NP8901 were there, along with twenty Royal Navy personnel. Every one of us was rapt with attention, listening as Boss Major Mike Norman pepped us up with a forceful plan of action.

Our Major was a strident man. We had already seen that he was given to stormy fits of bluster. His words as he paced back and forth came across as urgent and forceful.

To anyone who was listening, what came next was as clear as a bell.

"Today you are going to die," he roared ominously at the sea of blank faces staring back in his direction. "So go out there and do the job you were trained to do."

My heart sank a little bit. I was not ready to die. As I glanced sideways over at the chap next to me, a medic whose face was already as pale as a ghost, I realized that he felt the same way. I was only nineteen years old. Could this really be the end? There was nothing to be done, though, no protest. The order had been given. Now it was time to act.

A mixed mood took hold of the room. A sombre air captivated some of the faces, while others were aroused, seemingly ready to relish the coming fight. As Norman finished his rallying of the boys, the meeting broke up and everyone fell in line.

I bucked up, grabbing my kit and machine gun. One of my mates, Gaz, quipped as we hurried to join our section.

“No point in getting your head down now,” he said.

Gaz was right. We were the last and only line of defence 64 Royal Marines. All that stood between the Falklands Islands, a British territory for more than a century was in our ability to repel an uncertain army of invaders. The invaders were the elite Argentine Special Forces, the troops known as Buzo Tactico, had landed on the shores southwest of Stanley, near another settlement, Port Harriet.

They rumbled in larger numbers onto land, past Whalebone Cove in a line of LVTP-7’s, Amtrak personnel carriers. There were eighteen of the impressive American-made vehicles, each loaded with troops and equipped with .30 calibre machine guns.

The one hundred- and twenty-man invading force moved slowly up toward Sapper Hill before breaking off into two separate parties: the first moved into the hills, rounding back behind Government House, while the other headed directly toward the Marine barracks at Moody Brook, where they made their first, vicious attack.

By a little after six in the morning, those barracks where we had been given our orders were ablaze. The Buzo Tactico had been hopeful of catching us sleeping. They saturated the structure with heavy machine gun fire and phosphorous grenades. The attack was successful in destroying the structure, but they had arrived too late.

If the attack had come any earlier, the result would have been devastating. As the Moody Brook barracks burned to the ground a few kilometres northwest of Stanley, the attacking Argentine troops turned and began a trek toward the town. The unit that had first split into two halves would converse back together as one, clamping down like a vice around Government House.

The Marines had been successful in avoiding devastation at Moody Brook, but by now, Major Norman had to recognize what was going on. The Marine forces were outnumbered and badly outgunned. The guys in section two managed to pick off one of the Argentine LVTP-7's. A sharp-eyed marine managed to get off a shot from an anti-armor weapon, striking the passenger compartment. Others opened fire on the Amtrak, stopping it in its tracks. Section two may have slowed down the advancing vehicle, but this only served to make things worse. A fleet of Argentine vehicles emptied their troops, giving them cover as they moved forward, machine guns blasting.

As dawn crept closer, skirmishes like these broke out all over the island. The Marines fiercely engaged the invaders. The determined soldiers fought as long and as valiantly as they could. Backs against the walls though, each movement seemed to send them scrambling for a new position while the Argentine invaders dug in and fortified.

Scattered gunfire was exchanged between riflemen. Here and there, a lucky sniper caught a foot soldier, racing through the morning. British forces were able to fight in brief, intense periods, but they only managed to delay the advance before falling back. Our purpose was to defend the islands for as long as possible, either to repel them or scatter them far enough to regroup; we were largely unsuccessful on both fronts.

Major Norman had been caught with his pants down. All of the British troop positions were defending against an attack from the northeast; the Argentines had invaded the island from the opposite direction. Quickly, Norman called sections one and five back into Stanley and ordered them to retreat all the way back to Government House, where he too would hole up and prepare for his next move.

At 0615, the second branch of the Buzo Tactico party began their attack on the Government House complex. Argentine soldiers came down from the hills, approaching through a field at the rear of the complex. Six made it that far and made a bold attempt to enter the rear of Government House. Three were shot dead by defending Marines; the other three hid out in the Maid's Quarters in an outbuilding behind the main house. The hand full of Marines in the building managed to repel the rest of the Buzo Tactico, holding them off with rifle and machine gun fire.

Norman had made a request for support, but only roughly five minutes had passed since his call; not nearly enough time for sections one and five to help secure headquarters. Another wave of Argentine attackers, and the building could fall.

Gunfire volleyed all around the old building. As Norman scrambled back into the building, he found he was cut off. There were only thirty-one Royal Marines, eleven sailors from the HMS Endurance, and an former-Marine named Jim Fairfield left to defend the entire seat of government on the Falkland Islands. Between gunfire bursts, they could hear shouts in the trees. The next wave of Argentine forces drew nearer.

As the sun rose, the British position could be delicately described as precarious. In the heat of a fire fight, two factors must take hold in order for a soldier to survive the ordeal. The first is an ability to push through exhaustion and pain, or a shot of adrenaline; the second is the ability to seamlessly access their training.

Even though we were outnumbered and badly outgunned, the combat numbers were impressive. According to reports, there was somewhere close to six hundred Argentine soldiers lurking in the hills around Government House. Less than a hundred British soldiers defended the island.

Every one of the Royal Marines, who listened to Major Mike Norman's talk the night before survived the fire fight. Estimates said that we had managed to kill between twenty and thirty of their guys in the process. Even though the word of war spread at a snail's pace in 1982 compared to what it does now, it still did not take long to reach the opposing governments. The image of a dozen British Royal Marines, face down on the rock road with Argentine soldiers prowling up their backs, machine guns pointed, got blood boiling throughout the United Kingdom.

Quite a number of decades had passed since the British army had encountered the dilemma of having prisoners of war - what to do and how to negotiate their release. It hadn't been since the Second World War, when the POWs numbered in the thousands, that the question had been asked. Our defeat at Government House in Stanley presented Prime Minster Thatcher, and her cabinet, a whole new set of diplomatic problems.

Royal Marine training doesn't tell you precisely what to do when captured, but the implication should be clear. Maintain a strong stance, put up a wall of defiance. Do not say a word. Don't give the enemy anything to use against you.

On Monday, April 5th, roughly seventy-two hours after Government House fell to the squads of Argentine commandos; the HMS Invincible set sail out of Portsmouth. She regaled in patriotic glory, cutting through the chop with the Hermes along her side. The pictures were broadcast wide across the Empire and are quite staggering to behold. The massive ship, with flags unfurled, set against the morning sun. Sailing during spring in the Northern Hemisphere, she was escorted by a crowd of happy onlookers, people waving from yacht decks and fishing boats while passing through the narrow channel, under the shadow of Southsea Castle, out of harbour. Their departure was a clear sign of force.

As the men of NP8901 stepped off of the plane, onto the Brize Norton airstrip, the welcome we got proved to be quite glorious. It was one befitting a group of returning heroes; no one waving, and cheering saw us as losers. Perhaps they all knew what command was in store for us.

At the centre of our welcome party was Sir Stuart Robert Pringle, a Commandant General of the Royal Marines. Everyone knew Pringle or had at least heard his story. Pringle had joined the Marines in the year after World War II ended and quickly rose to become something of a titanic figure in the 45 Commando. Only six months before the Falkland conflict, in October 1981, Pringle had been severely wounded, losing his leg in an IRA bombing of his car outside of his Dulwich, South London home. He was lucky to be alive. The story famously goes that he was headed out for a run with his dog, Bella, and, on regaining his composure, asked his rescuer bravely, "How is my dog?"

An attendant brought Pringle out onto the stage in his wheelchair, where he bravely prepared to deliver an address.

All the lads in NP8901 stood in awe of the wounded hero, but when the moment came for our greeting, Pringle did us an unexpected turn. The dignified man stood out of his chair and beamed out upon us.

Given that an amphibious assault would be necessary, the Royal Marines were heavily involved. 3 Commando Brigade was brought to full combat strength, with not only 40, 42 and 45 Commandos, but also the 2nd and 3rd Battalions of the Parachute Regiment attached. The troops were landed at San Carlos Water at the western end of East Falkland, and preceded to “yomp" across the entire island to the capital, Stanley, which fell on 14 June 1982. Not only was 3 Commando Brigade deployed, but also a Royal Marines divisional headquarters, under Major-General Jeremy Moore, who was commander of British land forces during the war.

The Falkland Island War ended forty odd years ago. That's a lifetime for some men, those unlucky enough to have been buried down there. Thinking back on those frozen images, I simply cannot recall all of the names. A few stand out, but just as many have escaped me. Even those I do remember; I hardly know the fate of half of those lads.

A few days after the Argentinean forces surrendered on the Falkland Islands, June 20th, Two and a half months can go by in the blink of an eye; for me, it went quicker.

On the morning of April 2nd, 1982, I had been forced face down onto the cold courtyard stone outside the front steps of Government House. My weapon had been seized. My hands were up. A bunch of Argentinean commandos, mugging for the camera, surrounded my prone form. That was a dubious moment, not just in my life, but in the proud course of British history as well.

All the lads of NP8901, in that picture had been seething ever since, and it was on June 17th that we finally got the chance to restore order.

The moment started off in an ordinary fashion, where we were to gather in the courtyard. Just like always, we followed, trudging back out into the bracing cold, where a Union Jack awaited us.

It was then that I recognized what would come next.

Out of the small crowd of waiting Royal Marines and Navy personnel, the lads of NP8901 were called out to the front. Moments from glory, we gathered at the base of the flagpole.

There was no big band on the scene to stir our hearts. Nobody stood on ceremony, nor did anyone utter a patriotic word of cheer to mark the historic moment.

We attached the flag to its lanyard and raised it high into the sky. Then we stood back and watched it rippling in the wind.

All the books about the Falkland Island War show that moment: a group, bog-splattered Royal Marines clamouring to get their filthy hands on the dangling lanyard.

I do clearly recall, though, that the moment felt surprisingly good. NP8901 had all come full circle. Look it up. Look at the picture. You can see me right there.

At the same time tensions in the Middle East had reached a fevered pitch. On June 6th, after repeated skirmishes with the Palestine Liberation Organization, the PLO, Israeli forces invaded southern Lebanon. The invasion sparked the

Lebanon War. Rumors spread like wildfire that we would be re-routed to Israel to help the Israelis fight their war. British forces had backed the Israelis in territorial conflicts before; it seemed feasible that we would come to their aid now as well.

Israel in June sounded warm, almost inviting, compared to the God forsaken wind and rain of the Falkland Islands. No one wanted any part of that fight though. Those rumours began to rage out of control, and there was no impulse to quell them.

All the way back to the UK we talked drank and drank more beer trying to forget what just happened.

It was a lovely summer day in Portsmouth when we arrived back from the Falklands. An impressive crowd started gathering there along the docks to greet the Canberra early that morning. The cheers were loud. Happy mothers and children waved frantically from the docks, leaning out hopeful for a first look at their returning loved ones. We could see the colourful banners streaming in the breeze from a few kilometres out. It was breath-taking. We got our deserved dose of all the glittering pomp and circumstance afforded to returning victors.

Every Marine who served in the Falklands as part of NP8901 that year 1982 shared a similar fear. We all were pained with the thought that we would be sent back. Considering the circumstance, this fear was not an unfounded one; most of us were; after all, on a year's deployment there, and out of that, only six months had passed by. We very well could have ended up on that wind swept rock for the remaining six months, serving out our sentence as a garrison.

As it turns out though, I would never go back to the Falkland Islands.

When I returned to base that morning, I learned that NP8901 had been dissolved. As a result, we were ordered to put our names in for a draft. All right, I thought. We've been spared that awful fate.

The Royal Marines have a recruitment company, R-Company, as it is commonly referred to. Marines serving in that company travel out to all the little country towns, wearing polished boots and their dress uniforms. They shake hands and tell every one of those adoring people what it's like to serve in the RMC; they're a well-armed PR firm; they wanted to bring in a few young lads who had served in the Falklands, making our bright smiling faces seem like the perfect candidates. R-Company is quite competitive though; only thirty or so lads serve there at a time, I deserved a cushy number and I wanted to stay in Poole, where the summers are like heaven.

my thoughts rarely drifted back to the Falkland Islands. What happened to me there came out as stories, tossed around the bar with the other Royal Marines. That was all they were to me, stories just tossed around for laughs.

There was only once I can recall when I had "a moment." I was traveling through Argentina with my girlfriend at the time. We were in Buenos Aires when we came across the Argentinean memorial to the fallen soldiers of Guerra de las Malvinas.

I needed to catch my breath. Although I made the obvious connection being in Argentina, the memorial unexpectedly stirred all those memories back up again. Then it was gone. I choked it back and moved on. It has been that way for thirty-nine years now. Memories of war resurface in glimmers, only to be forced back down.

I only lasted a few months in R-Coy before getting kicked out for performing at a show, but that's another story, I got a draft up to 45 Commando, Scotland in the summer months of 1983 just in time to witness the beautiful Scottish summer.

Arbroath, 45 Commando

45 Commando has or had a reputation for being the 'Bad boy' unit, stuck up on their own in Scotland. Arbroath town disliked most of the young Marines who frequented the bars trying to get their girls, especially English lads like me.

45 Commando (pronounced 'Four Five Commando') is an amphibious commando unit within 3 Commando Brigade. The Commando base located 2 miles northwest of the centre of Arbroath in E Angus, RM Condor

began as a Fleet Air Arm facility, which was established in 1938, and later became a Royal Naval Air Station, known as HMS Condor. The home of 45 Commando since 1971, Condor has a complement of almost 900 military and civilian personnel.

I joined 'Y' Company or Yankee as its known, 5 troop, just in time for my very first Mountain training followed by my first Norway.

Mountain training was difficult, not because of the mountains but because of the rain which came at you horizontally. We all had to undergo unit mountain training, with extensive exercises focusing on navigation and conditioning for the Arctic in the Highlands, where temperatures have plummeted to a cool -15°c.

It's all staged out of Cameron Barracks in Inverness and consists of vertical assault techniques, traversing ridges using fixed lines, winter skill training (using ice axes and crampons), obstacle crossing, river cross skills.

It doesn't end there, with cold weather warfare survival, first aid, casualty evacuation, specialist cold weather equipment training also built into the program to form the building blocks for a successful winter deployment. All of this training is delivered by Recce Troop and has seen us all carry out a tactical crossing of An Teallach Mountain, nicknamed the great wilderness, and navigation routes on the Fannichs range. Yankee Company were the lucky ones, getting the first of this winter's snow during our winter training package, facing gusts of wind of 50mph and a wind chill of -15°c.

It's this sort of training that will make 5 troop more resilient when we're in Norway on Northern Wedding '86.

Those new to the Arctic must undergo a series of intensive trials to ensure they are able to survive one is the Cold shock ice-breaking drill That involves being plunged into a hole in the ice and climbing out of the water unassisted using ski poles.

As well as learning how to Ski and having to know how to get into battle and move around during combat in one of the planet's most unforgiving environments, where the sun barely rises and temperatures plummet to below -30C. It includes building shelters, digging snow holes, and surviving.

We must be able to carry weights of up to 75lbs; pulling pulks (sleds) weighing up to 40lb through the snow on skis. Much of the training includes cross-country ski marches of up to 20 kilometres a day, alpine skiing, we did get the Saturday morning to go downhill skiing which was far more exciting and less exhausting.

The Aurora Borealis painted a breath-taking arc of light across the Arctic skies where I found myself in a tent high in the Norwegian wilderness under a 10-man tent sheet, where the snow is the ground sheet; this was just one insight into learning the art of survival in cold weather warfare. Surviving an arctic ration pack with 5000 calories a day needed to operate in this harsh environment, was an operation in its self.

I had to learn how to survive, to manoeuvre and ultimately fight in one of the most inhospitable terrains on earth, because they say that you can soldier here, you can soldier anywhere.

My first Norway was hard with Yankee Company, but well worth the experience gained as I moved on to join the Recce troop for my next winter deployment which was totally different and involved more technical operations, beach landings using the Rigid Raiding Craft, Used in extremes of climate conditions from -30°C to +40 °C. the standard light assault craft is 5.2 meters long and was first developed in the 1970s as a Beach Raider. The 5.2 meter Mk I Raiding Craft fitted with a 140 Hp single outboard petrol engine, giving a speed of 37 knots light and 31 knots laden with 4 fully kitted Royal Marines and one coxswain for beach recces and beach assaults. Mountain routing and start lines for attacks on enemy positions advanced operations involving parachuting behind enemy lines.

Royal Marines undergo military parachute training at RAF Brize Norton without having to undergo P-Company training with the Parachute Regiment. This allows flexibility of insertion methods for all force elements.

All of Recce troop members had been Para trained and generally, parachute training when in Arbroath was from a static line suspended from a balloon set up on the airfield. The balloon was set to 800 feet we were told a descent from a static balloon at 800ft would take just 28 seconds. One drops vertically for a hundred feet until the chute opens with a loud bang, I prayed "God bless the WAAF who packed it " when the wind started to blow we have jumped from as low as 600 feet, which does not give much time to pull a reserve if needed. Although we did get regular jumps tailgating from the C130 onto to the airfield used purely as a drop zone, for the Hercules aircraft operating out of RAF Leuchars, sometimes 5 jumps per day which was intense. We would all get on a bus for the journey from Condor in Arbroath the a one hour trip taking the scenic route along the east coast down through Carnoustie and Dundee , over the bridge to RAF Leuchars, before boarding the plane for a ten minute flight before jumping out either onto the airfield or a place called ‘Barry buddon’ which is not really ideal for landings as it’s a combination of sand dunes and gauze bushes, and when you are getting dragged through those at a rapid rate of knots it’s not very comfortable.

Royal Marines are trained to operate in a demanding and dangerous environment. Their training is intended to develop fortitude. Exceptional performance is superfluous but consistent performance, whatever the conditions, is required. Royal Marines must have the fortitude to carry out tasks when they are tired and when the tasks seem almost overwhelming. They must have the moral courage to persist. Commando units rely above all upon the ability of their members simply to endure.

We never spent much time back on the base as the unit was committed to deployments like Norway every year for three months, then Northern Ireland for six months, only to return to Norway again so not much time to feel the anti-English attitude in the small town.

But when in Rome, I did enjoy being one of a very few English Marines drinking in the small Scottish town, never a dull night. We used to drink in a bar called The Golden Quaich, the word Quaich meaning, Scotland's cup of friendship, which has been used through the centuries to offer a welcoming drink at clan gatherings, and other family occasions, and to friends and visitors. Let me tell you, there was not any welcome in that bar especially if you happened to be English. There were plenty of antics to be seen and comprising acts such as exposing yourself, urinating in public, drinking each other's urine, smacking bare buttocks, and committing acts of a graphic sexual nature, all part of the fun back in the day, along with a good fight and a night of debauchery with one of the local girls which inevitably ended up with a trip to Dundee on Monday morning to attend the 'dose' clinic at Ninewells hospital.

A quick glance from the doctor confirming what you already knew, that you had Gonorrhoea just looking at the dripping dick. Issued with the medication and the instructions not to drink while on antibiotics and away you went to the nearest bar for an all-day drinking session in Dundee.

Time rolls on, and after three winter deployments it was time to start training for our deployment to Northern Ireland on Operation Banner.

Pre-Deployment Training

From 1969 onwards Royal Marine units regularly deployed to Northern Ireland during The Troubles.

Basic training for a tour of Northern Ireland is undertaken 6 miles west of Folkstone, on the edge of the town of Hythe, off the A259 Hythe-Dymchurch-Hastings's Road. An area of low lying, slightly undulating land was adjoining the foreshore. Hythe Ranges is one of the oldest ranges in the country and has been used for live firing for nearly 200 years. During the live firing and afterwards was the time to collect spare live ammo, 7.62mm, for deployment too Northern Ireland, as spare ammo just in case! The whole area is steeped in military history. There are two Martello Towers on Hythe Ranges, and a “Grand Redoubt” fortification at Dymchurch. These were built in the early 1800s to resist potential invasion by Napoleon.

Pre-tour training was formalized, largely under NITAT at Hythe and Lydd. This quickly became NITAT UKLF when a second team was established at Sennelager in Germany. These teams trained units deploying to Northern Ireland for residential or Roulement tours. A Northern Ireland Reinforcement Training Team (NIRTT) was established in theatre to train individuals on trickle postings, or those joining unit's mid-tour. Attendance at NITAT or NIRTT was mandatory for all individuals posted to Northern Ireland.

The Training teams had first-hand knowledge and real credibility. The great majority of instructors from colour sergeants to captains, had just completed an operational tour in theatre themselves. The training team leaders, captains had the personality, knowledge, and credibility to lead through experience.

During the Troubles, the British armed forces constructed and used an already erected mock towns and streets to replicate the urban environment that troops would experience during tours of Northern Ireland. We went to Lydd and Hythe and then to the Ballykinler camp in Co Down, was situated in the North.

staged "riots" on the training ground in Lydd, in which we complete with riot gear and a Saxon armoured vehicles by confronting a gang of off duty Royal Marines dressed as civilians throwing stones and petrol bombs to simulate a real riot.

We are confronted with a barrage of petrol bombs, missiles, and abuse during Northern Ireland training at Lydd. Simulated riots tested the teamwork, discipline, and courage of the Royal Marines as we practiced how to work together to defend each other and drive back unruly angry and potentially harmful crowds. having missiles, petrol bombs and a lot of verbal abuse thrown at you gets the adrenaline going making you ready for anything.

A riot is a noisy and stressful environment, and it's a valuable experience to have been exposed to it and establish control, we must work together and make sure we look after each other. It's important and a real challenge to keep your calm and match the aggression that's presented to you, so as not to worsen the situation. We had plenty of aggression, for me the best part was the 'snatch squad' when the shields opened and two of us ran out to grab a person identified as a leader or instigator or organizer and drag them back behind the shields for arrest and release.

In the past the box formation during a riot had worked where the major tactic was to shoot the ringleaders. This was not considered appropriate in Northern Ireland and therefore arrest, or ‘snatch’ squads were used. The Box was found to be un-maneuverable and made it difficult for snatch squads to exit and re-enter quickly. In addition, the Box presented a quite easy target for gunmen. The forces rapidly adapted to a combination of manned shield walls and snatch squads. The gunman threat was countered by placing marksmen on roofs and in upper stories. For planned operations, teams of marksmen were infiltrated behind the main body of the rioters. The marksmen would make their presence known once the riot had fully developed, making it difficult for any gunmen to make a getaway.

The next response to riot training was baton rounds which were rubber, but these were relatively ineffective because the range at which they would knock a man off his feet was less than the range of a brick or petrol bomb. The first generation of polypropylene baton rounds was not much better. The later generation of more powerful polypropylene baton rounds were certainly effective but ran an increased risk of serious injury to the rioters especially when fired ten feet before the target aimed at the road so it would bounce up and hit the target at a much higher velocity, much like a cricket ball during a bouncer. On occasion the polypropylene rounds were replaced with double D batteries by some thugs within the unit. The need to have non-lethal weapons in the Army's armoury was clear before the Northern Ireland Campaign; the lesson was that a process of research and development for such weapons is required in order that effectiveness can be maintained. Large-scale rioting was eventually countered by a combination of measures: skilful siting of shield walls; containing the riot on the rioters' home ground threatening the rear of the rioting body with mobile patrols; allowing routes for the rioters to disperse; and limited use of CS and baton rounds to keep the rioters at an appropriate distance.

Back in the 80's petrol bombers were a threat to life and therefore a legitimate target for opening fire under the Yellow Card. The counters to petrol bombers were a combination of baton rounds (to keep the petrol bomber at a distance) and the deployment of fire extinguishers behind shield walls.

Training awareness of the threat and good drills, all part of the Lydd experience. The terrorist threat to the Royal Marines was primarily a combination of gunmen and bombs. Improvised mortars were a threat to static installations, particularly after the development of the Mark 10, which was first used in 1979 but not deployed in large numbers until 1985.There were three main kinds of Improvised Explosive Devise, IEDs: Radio Controlled IEDs (RCIED); Command Wire IEDs (CWIED); and Victim Operated IEDs (VOIED), booby-traps. Time-delay fused Improvised Explosive Devises were also used, particularly early in the campaign, but the lack of man-in the-loop control presented problems for the bombers. In remarkably simple terms, RCIEDs could be defeated by electronic countermeasures, ECM; CWIEDs could be defeated by photographic reconnaissance, planned searches, rummage searches and other aspects of patrol tactics; and VOIEDs could be defeated by a high level of awareness of the threat and good drills (such as checking under cars before using them). The effectiveness of all IEDs was to some extent reduced by good drills, particularly by avoiding bunching. After 1980 very few IEDs killed or wounded more than one or two soldiers at a time.

NITAT and NIRTT ensured that all troops deploying to theatre were professionally trained and briefed as to what to expect in Northern Ireland. The professional standards set, and achieved in a few weeks of training, were high. Pre-tour training saved lives and was a ‘war winner’.

During this training we got handed and trained in the use of the ‘Yellow card’ which was the guidance for opening fire, not liked by the Marines on the ground, if a terrorist fired at you, you could fire back but if he stopped firing and ran away, we could not fire at him to stop his getaway.

‘The Yellow Card’. The Card itself has no force in law but seeks to reflect the law of self-defence and identify the circumstances when potentially lethal force may be used. It was effectively the Rules of Engagement for most operational circumstances. It was intended that so long as soldiers adhered to the contents of the Yellow Card then they would be acting within the law; and that was proven to be the case. The Card was subjected to continuous review and scrutiny, but since it was written with legal purposes in mind it was not generally found to be user friendly, at least in the early days. What seemed to be required was some form of situational trainer who taught us to shout, "Stop or I fire"?

It is meant to fit into a pocket, so that we have it with us the whole time. The problem is, when in a contact, we cannot get the card and think, "Oh, what can I do?" It had to be remembered. It must be built into your mind, what should I do in a case where we might use firearms. It must be instinctive.

So that we understood the rules, there was a lot of instruction on pre-operational tour training. The rules were clear and precise as to what we could and could not do.

This had to be in your mind: We were to use minimum force in all situations, and open fire only as a last resort.

Although 'No' live rounds were to be carried in the breech unless we were ordered otherwise or were about to fire, many did chamber a round and then once back in the barracks accidently fire the round into the unloading bay or even worse into himself or an oppo standing next to him. The ND or negligent discharge would then cost the person a £200 fine. I still remember my first lesson on Weapon Safety. The corporal teaching us began by saying, "More British soldiers have died as a result of an ND than the IRA, managed to kill in Northern Ireland."

Challenges were always to be given before firing, unless to do so would increase the risk of death or grave injury to us or anyone we considered was being engaged by terrorists.

Challenges were to be clear: “Marines. Stop or I fire!”

We were ordered to open fire only if someone was committing an act likely to endanger life and there was no other way to stop them. Only aimed shots were to be fired; no more rounds than necessary were to be fired; and be careful not to hit anyone who is innocent.

Those rules were drilled into all of us. We practiced them. We spent ages in a classroom learning them. We also practiced scenarios in exercises and were judged on whether we had done the right thing.

Camera surveillance in support of military operations

Off to Beaconsfield for a two-week course to Carry out Personnel Recognition Photography as part of the COP training program we as a team of four had to Demonstrate the types of, and the detail required in photographs used to support personnel recognition. Demonstrate the types of material and objects which can be used as cover to take photographs and not be seen. Demonstrate the techniques for photographing a moving person. Carry out vehicle Recognition photography and the detail required in photographs used to support vehicle recognition. Demonstrate the techniques for photographing a moving vehicle.

Carry out photography to show detail in property. Demonstrate types of, and the detail required in photographs used to show detail of property. Demonstrate the techniques for photographing property. Carry out Panoramic photography. Demonstrate the techniques required for panoramic photography.

Demonstrate competency in producing Covert and Overt photographs. Produce Covert photographs of personnel Produce Covert photographs of vehicles Produce panoramic photographs of open ground and buildings.

Demonstrate the techniques of focusing the SLR camera Describe the shutter, aperture relationship. Describe and demonstrate the effects of shutter, aperture combinations on depth of field demonstrate the effects of shutter, aperture combinations on depth of field. Describe the methods of determining exposure. Demonstrate the methods of determining exposure,

Identify the main factors which determine photographic Composition, common photographic faults attributable to incorrect camera operation. Rectify common photographic faults attributable to incorrect camera operation. Practical training and assessment conducted in classrooms and in-situ in the training environment under simulated conditions found in the operational environment.

My favourite part of the course was the development of the film The first step in preparing to develop film is to set up your workspace and gather all materials required before turning the lights off, you need complete darkness once the development process begins.

Taking out the film and putting in the film tank has to be done in complete darkness, once that's done the fun starts Since your film is safe in your film tank, you can now turn on the lights to complete the next steps. The developer mixture is used to develop film negatives in the tank, and the exact amount will vary depending on the size of the film tank. Mix the two ingredients in a metal or plastic container then pour into the film tank and shake.

After using fixer, your film reel is safe to remove from the tank. You then rinse the film with cold water for a few minutes to ensure they are no leftover chemicals. Next, soak your film in a wetting agent to help rid it of excess water and avoid developing streak. The room now has a very addictive smell and makes the process enjoyable when hanging, drying and printing. The only disappointing part is when the photos come out not exactly as you saw them when taking the photo!

From the top of the white cliffs of dover, looking down onto the ferry terminal over one mile away Apply the long lens,2000mm Apply the rules of composition Determine exposure, depth of field. Produce a panorama of the people leaving the ferry. We also completed a video and sound course which involved walking around Windsor castle interviewing people and the techniques used to conduct interviews using a hand held video camera.

Walking around the small town of Windsor in two's armed with a mike and camera we approached every pretty girl on the street asking for an interview, but really wanting to get a date later that night.

Moving on from the UK, later we had to demonstrate the same skills Using the same equipment only this time from the Mourne mountains where we Produced Covert photographs of personnel and Covert photographs of vehicles, we also Produced panoramic photographs of open ground and buildings situated in the small towns being overlooked by the mountains.

Operating out of the Ballykinler camp which was known as a soft area and is situated on the southeast coast of Northern Ireland, right on the coast with a blue flag beach overlooked by the Mourne Mountains. Well you say soft area we did encounter loud explosions while operating from the hill, whether they were planned or accidental we will never know but we know Cpl Brian Brown of the UDR, was Killed by an IRA bomb as he and his search dog Oliver, made a second search of a petrol station, on the Newry Road, Kilkeel, after a bomb warning. A colleague was badly injured, his dog was killed. A dog handler for ten years, Corporal Brown had declined promotion because he wanted to continue working with dogs. He had received a GOC's

Commendation in 1983 which read, 'his professionalism made an excellent impression on regular units who have come to rely on his advice with complete assurance'. He was awarded a Posthumous Queen's Gallantry Medal which the Queen presented to his widow in Jul 1987. He was 37 years old, on duty and Married at the time of his death on the 28th of May 1986. This may have been the loud explosion we heard from the camp.

Recce Troop

The Reconnaissance Troop, or Recce Troop, is an element of the Headquarters Company of 45 Commando. Recce Troops are highly specialized units, each manned by some 28 Royal Marines, with many trained as Reconnaissance Operators (ROs) and Mountain Leaders (MLs). As the name indicates, a Recce Troop's role is to carry out reconnaissance for its parent Commando. This task may involve operating behind enemy lines to gather intelligence on enemy forces and preparing the way for the main force.

A Recce Troop consists of 4-man teams, each led by a Sergeant or Corporal, typically a Mountain Leader.

Royal Marines wishing to join the troop must pass the Recce Troop Selection Course. Becoming a Reconnaissance Operator in a Recce Troop is a good grounding towards becoming a Mountain Leader. 2 tours in a Recce Troop enable COP selection. Recce Troop Royal Marines are parachute trained. The success of the mission depends on knowing where and how strong the enemy is. As a Reconnaissance Operator, it'll be your job to find out. You are trained in climbing and cliff-assault techniques, allowing you to gather vital intelligence and get it back to your unit in total secrecy.

Recce Troops also include a sniper section, manned by Royal Marines with the Platoon Weapons 3 (PW3) specialization. Their role is to engage the enemy with long range accurate sniper fire and to gather intelligence.

Recce Troop snipers deploy as 2-man teams of shooter and spotter. Recce Troop sniper teams were frequently attached to each one of the Commando's rifle companies to provide them with sniper cover.

The sniper rifle most wielded by a Recce Troop Sniper Team shooter is the L115A3 Long Range Rifle. They may also carry a SA80A2 rifle as a personal weapon and a sig Sauer 9mm pistol as a sidearm. In some situations, the shooter may instead use the L121A1 .50 calibre anti-material rifle. The spotter element of a sniper team will carry a L129a1 Sharpshooter rifle or SA8A2 and a 9mm pistol. The spotter may use various scopes and imaging systems such as a spotting scope, binoculars, and thermal imaging devices. Night vision attachments for the sniper rifle and spotter's optics will be used for night ops. The team may also be armed with various grenades and a LASM rocket launcher, not in Northern Ireland back in 1986.

Our Recce troop enjoyed the reputation as being the best in the corps, the best and the bad as we used to be known, the year before on July 13, 1985. Recce troops from 40 and 42 commando joined up for a Parachute exercise using Sea King helicopters off the west coast of Scotland, on the Isle of Lewis and Isle of Harris which form the main island in the Outer Hebrides. On the Isle of

Lewis, the summers are short, cool, and windy; the winters are long, very cold, wet, and extremely windy; and it is mostly cloudy year-round. Wind is not good when parachuting, believe me, when you hit the deck and get dragged over rocks the size of small cars.

During the day we had been battered as we hit the rocky outcrops, leaving everyone with bruises and sprains. The boss managed to get the lads the night off for a drink in Stornoway, the main town on the island of Lewis. To get into town we got a lift from one of the chopper pilots in his, Sea King adapted by Westland as a troop transport and was known as the Commando. who dropped our troop off in a school playground, one lift at a time, which must have been an odd sight for the locals at the time.

We had no idea that on that night 'Live aid' was being broadcast around the world, a worldwide rock concert organized to raise money for the relief of famine-stricken Africans. Including a bar in Stornoway where we found ourselves surrounded by incredibly angry locals wanting to cause bodily harm to the Marines for trying to steal away their girls. A running fight through the small streets followed by a tactical retreat running towards a waiting chopper much like the scene from Saigon where the Marines piled into the chopper. The last man scrambled aboard before it left Saigon behind in back in1975 captured on film by Hugh Van a reporter there at the time. Once all the lads made it to the chopper the pilot got it up into the air, on our way back to the base we used on Harris, everyone started on a debrief, what just happened?

The next morning, I stood supporting a black eye and sore head ready to jump from the Sea king feeling like shit.

shuffle along the chopper floor on your arse, wanting the fresh air to hit you and bring some relief from the cramped position and heavy kit strapped to your leg then, the weightless feeling brings a grin back to your face as you hurl towards to ground at 122 miles per hour.

Proper landing procedures consist of executing a parachute landing fall to dissipate the forces of ground contact because it appeared to reduce the injury risk compared with earlier landing methods. It begins with the feet and knees together, toes pointed toward the ground, and knees slightly bent and rotated to the side. The upper extremities are raised with the forearms held tightly in front of the face, and the chin is tucked. As the feet contact the ground the Marine rolls sideways and sequentially onto the outer side of the legs, thighs, buttocks, and trunk. He then rolls onto his back to complete the landing.

All the pain comes back when you hit the ground with a jolt and start to release the chute before getting dragged over the rocky outcrops at a rapid rate of knots.

Airborne training operations are discontinued when winds are greater than 13 knots. Wind increases horizontal drift and parachute oscillations. When horizontal velocity from drift and oscillation are added to the vertical descent velocity, ground impact forces are elevated, and landing control may be compromised; these factors may lead to a higher injury risk. Winds can push a jumper away from pre-planned drop zones into obstacles, rougher terrain, or trees. High winds also dragged the Marines on the ground after they land and before they have time to collapse their parachute canopies.

After one jump we had been battered that much the boss halted the day giving us time to recover and re-group ready for the following day. With the day off I decided to have a walk around the island trying to find one of the abandoned houses which looked like a time capsule screaming to be photographed. A one bar electric fire, an Aga iron, a clothes mangle, all paint a vivid picture of the life in the past century yet fading with every passing storm. There is often a unique sense of presence in these places, not necessarily in the form of a spirit or a ghost, but just in the fact that the occupants never had a chance to properly leave, so a part of them remains. One of the items I saw lying around was a Bible open on a bedside cabinet there was a suitcase packed as though someone was about to go on holiday in the 1970s but for some reason never got the chance.

I found some good clues as to when they were last occupied. One had an insurance certificate lying on a table next to an empty envelope as though it had just been opened. It expired in Oct 1979. Another house had a newspaper dated July 10th, 1983, with the headline "Death Penalty - A Last Chance?". One had a newspaper dated 1960 but it didn’t feel abandoned that long ago as the decor looked decisively late 70s or early 80s. Maybe the occupant was a fashion guru ahead of their time.

A particularly chilling house I entered had all the personal belongings still in place. Ornamental handheld mirrors, perfume sprays and pin cushions all artfully arranged on a lace mat atop a dressing table occupied one bedroom as though the occupant had just popped down the shops, that morning after making themselves look presentable. Yet in the meantime, all the wallpaper had fallen off the walls and a few birds had died on the floor. In the same room, dresses were hanging in the wardrobe as though waiting to be taken off their hangers and worn again. I didn't try them on as they looked too big for me, and after all, it was only a Tuesday.

One particularly gruesome story about the same house was that the owner was clearly a cat lover. Porcelain cat figures adorned the fireplace in the lounge, and a mounted photo of a cat with a poem accompanying it took pride of place on the wall above probably a much-missed deceased pet. In the corner of the bedroom where the dresses were hanging in the wardrobe was the skeletal remains of a cat and strewn around the place were other signs of more cats having died in the property too. My guess was that the owner had passed away and her beloved cats had been left to fend for themselves, unloved, until they starved themselves to a long and slow death.

These houses are sadly suffering the same fate slowly being starved because of being left behind and forgotten about. Their fate happens on a much longer scale than the cats (which hopefully wasn't too long), but somewhere along their timeline of demise they become works of living art, and a perfect subject for an unusual genre of photography. Armed with my 'Nikon FA' I spent the day taking some great photos to remember the bleak and eerie homes of Harris.

After an eventful two weeks the three recce troops went their own way and we moved back to Arbroath ready for Mountain training and the Norway deployment, early 86'.

Norway 1986 winter deployment

45 Commando deployed to Norway conducting essential training as the Lead Commando Unit every year. As Cold Weather Warfare specialists held at extremely high readiness, training is vital to retaining capability to deploy anywhere in the world in the event of crisis and to support NATO allies in the region.

Half the battle is managing the climate and the terrain. Snowstorms can occur suddenly, so learning the basics of survival is essential to operating in the Arctic conditions. The Cold Weather Warfare Course has three phases – survival, mobility, and warfare with a view to creating a well-rounded "winter warrior" or 'Arctic Fox', enabling the commandos to operate effectively in the unforgiving Arctic environment.

To get ready for the northern freeze, 45 Commando undergo unit mountain training, with extensive exercises focusing on navigation and conditioning for the Arctic in the Highlands of Scotland, where temperatures have plummeted to a cool -15°c.

All this training is delivered by 45 Commando's Recce Troop and has seen the commandos carry out a tactical crossing of An Teallach mountain, nicknamed the great wilderness, and navigation routes on the Fannichs range.

It falls on Recce troop to deliver this essential training to 45 Commando, who are held at high readiness to head on operations around the globe at a moment's notice.

Our team is here to train and ensure the commandos of the brigade can live, move, and fight in the mountains. This exercise is infamous for its difficulty. Fighting in the mountains is difficult. The resilience and mental strength of those who deploy will be tested from day one.

Training will push people out of their comfort zone. It's particularly challenging operating on ridge lines during these conditions with steep drops either side or a strong wind blowing, it can be daunting for some people. It's this sort of training that will make the team more resilient when in Norway.

During that winter of 1986, our team had been tasked to set up an OP above the tree line where the only cover given is the snow, so after digging our two-man tents into the deep snow during the night and settling into our routine of food and sleep. I started the 'watch' system where one tent, one man on watch and one tent off. Unfortunately, one tent fell asleep totally exhausted by the long ski up and into the observation post location, so the watch system failed.

The snow came down relentlessly during the few hours before Jim woke and started shouting, "wake up we are trapped" or words to that effect! Under the weight of the snow we couldn't move an inch, we were getting crushed slowly by the weight of snow.

Jim managed to wiggle his way out of the tent and started shovelling off the snow to release the smothering feeling and claustrophobic panic. Reflecting on the incident it could have been me who fell asleep, but no blame was apportioned as we had survived as a team and we carried on as a team.

The parachute training in Norway has its own issues, but still the best week of the whole 3-month deployment. Operating 200km inside the Arctic Circle with temperatures sinking below minus 30 The briefing mission began at Bardufoss Air Station in northern

Norway inside an aircraft hangar. Around 60 men stood in an half shell shape around a Captain wearing a green beret but a Para reg badge. He started his address to our Recce troop, 42 Recce a few Mountain leaders from brigade, men from the SAS & SBS and the pathfinders from the parachute regiments with these immortal words "Morning men, today the pathfinders will use the side exit (cumbersome and unorganized exit) as they are normal parachuting solders, while the rest will tailgate (off the back ramp of the plane) as they are special forces" well you should have seen their faces! we boarded a C-130 Hercules aircraft.

A static line is a cord attached to both the aircraft and the Marines' parachute. As he exits the aircraft, the cord automatically pulls open his pack that contains the parachute canopy, slowing his descent.

Risk factors for static-line parachuting injuries included night jumps, jumps with extra equipment, higher wind speeds, higher air temperatures, jumps from fixed-wing aircraft rather than balloons or helicopters, jumps onto certain types of terrain, greater body weight, simultaneous exits from both sides of an aircraft, Entanglements occur when the equipment of two or more jumpers becomes intertwined during descent. During exits from aircraft with 2 doors, high-altitude entanglements can occur with simultaneous exits from both sides of the aircraft. Whereas a 1-second delay is now required for jumps out of 2-door aircraft, this timing is difficult to maintain if a jumper on one side rushes the door or hesitates at it. In addition to high-altitude entanglements, there was also mid-altitude entanglements, after full canopy deployment its possible if 1 jumper drifts into another or if 1 jumper's parachute is directly on top of another. In the latter case, the higher jumper can land on top of the lower parachute. During training, para's are instructed to pull on their parachute risers to direct their parachutes away from other jumpers. However, mid-altitude entanglement may occur rapidly, and the jumper may not be aware until the situation occurs. Entanglements can substantially increase injury risk. Depending on the nature of the entanglement and the posture of the para's when the entanglement occurs, the situation can result in less controlled landings on ground contact. Winds, from the rear of the aircraft on exit entanglements or jumps involving a greater number of men or frozen rigging! our chutes had been packed back in the UK where the humidity was maybe high and contains water in the static rigging, once flown out to Norway into -20 below freezing, well that's what happened on day one.

We jumped as a stick of four men; all four had to pull their reserve as we hurtled towards the frozen ground covered by 20 foot of snow. The reserves opened at tree level , so we all escaped serious injuries that day.

Parachutes with larger canopies reduced the injury risk. Staggered exits from opposite sides of aircraft with 2 doors reduced injuries at altitude. Exits from tailgates reduced the injury risk. Entanglements among paratroopers substantially increased the risk of injury. In tailgate exits, static lines are attached to cables in a way that is less likely to produce static-line injuries. More space between jumpers likely reduces entanglements and injuries at altitude. Jumps with extra equipment typically involved loaded rucksacks, special weapons, this equipment can substantially increase the total weight on the parachute and result in a faster descent rate, leading to greater impact forces on ground contact.

Landing-zone characteristics like 20 foot of soft snow, jumps onto landing zones described as “frozen” due to uneven ground and obstacles, such as frozen lakes and drifting snow, on the rougher landing zones that make the proper execution of a landing difficult.

Jumps onto land had about 4 times the risk of jumps into snow, possibly due to the shock-absorbing quality of snow. However, in the possibilities of parachute entanglements and difficulties doffing heavy equipment that can pull the Marine deeper into the snow also his exist becomes a nightmare.

The weather was not within the limits for parachuting for most of the week, so we spent most of the time drinking and chasing beautiful Norwegian girls around town. After 3 months in the arctic circle, you are ready for some

R&R. First, we had to complete the final exercise Cold winter which covers land, sea and air elements. UK involvement focuses on maritime and will involve around 350 Royal Marines from 3 Commando Brigade working closely with Dutch marines. The Royal Marines are the UK's cold weather warfare specialists, and this exercise concludes our annual cold weather training period in Norway.

After returning to Scotland, we had a couple of weeks off before being sent to Germany on course.

International Long Range Reconnaissance Patrol School

Our Team of four, set out from Scotland and a train journey to the south of Germany, we had been enrolled on the Long-range patrol course, the Close combat course and as an extra we had to test the new sniper weapon made Heckler & Koch at their factory in Germany. Run by Special Operations Forces, trained in advanced individual patrolling, medical, close quarter battle, sniper, survival, planning, and recognition skills. It was established in 1979, and first called the International Long Range Reconnaissance Patrol School (ILRRPS)

The centre was started as centralisation of training for long range reconnaissance patrol units and Special Operation Forces. In a joint ,training facility in Europe. The first memorandum of understanding was signed on August 1, 1980, by Belgium, Germany, and the United Kingdom establishing the centre in Weingarten, Germany,

Our first task was a visit to the Heckler & Koch at their factory to test the sniper weapon, as a replacement for the British 7.62 mm L42A1 sniper weapon. The MSG90 is a sniper rifle. This weapon developed by Heckler & Koch in the mid 1980's as a lighter, cheaper, and more rugged alternative to the PSG-1. This makes the MSG90 better suited as for military use while retaining most of the qualities of the PSG-1. The maximum effective range of the MSG90 is 1.000 meters. With the proper ammunition.

Arriving at the factory we went straight to their indoor ranges to start firing various pistols and small arms weapons, like the P9 which is a semi-automatic pistol. It fires the 9x19mm round from a 9-round magazine from a 7-round magazine. The effective range is a few dozen meters.

We liked the VP70M which fires the 9x19mm parabellum from an 18 round detachable magazine. This model can be used in burst mode. Which requires the shoulder stock to be attached? The three round burst is fired at a cyclic rate of fire of 2.200 rpm. Maximum effective range is about 50 meters.

On to the famous MP5 which fires the 9x19mm round from 15 or 30 round magazines. The cyclic rate of fire is 800 rounds per minute. The production quality closed bolt operation and free-floating barrel result in a high accuracy. The maximum effective range of: one hundred too two hundred meters. The best part of all this live firing was we didn't have to load a single magazine as people loaded them as we fired.

My personal favourite was the MP5-K in a briefcase. With the trigger on the carry case handle which allows the weapon to be fired from within the case which in turn catches the spent rounds, thus leaving no evidence that a weapon has been fired. But like all the submachine guns in the world the rounds always start low and move upwards and to the right in a stream of rounds, so fired from the knee position I doubt that you would hit your target, unless you positioned the case exactly on the body you required to hit!

Treating the four Marines as buyers they then 'wined and dined' us I suppose the UK armed forces purchasing their 'Sniper weapon' would be quite a coup. While I enjoyed firing the MSG90 out to a 1000m, Jim and Taff, the two snipers had issues with the weight. Jim was used to L42A1 weight of 5.67kg which he could move into position using movement techniques like the low crawl, medium crawl, high crawl, hand-and-knees crawl, into the Final Firing Position (FFP) maintaining good concealment during the entire movement.

The 6.3kg of the MSG90 in Jim's opinion was not ideal; he voiced his opinion in his report back to HQ, weather that report made the decision to go with the L96 we will never know. L96 the sniper rifle produced by Accuracy International derived from their PM rifle which was designed by Olympic marksman Malcolm Cooper. This weapon was adopted into British Service in the early 1980s as a replacement for the Lee–Enfield L42. The L96 in turn was replaced by the Accuracy International .338 Lapua Magnum L115A3 rifle.

The L115A3 bolt-action rifle was developed to have an effective range of 1,500 to 1,700 meters—compared to that of the .50 BMG cartridges. The .338 Lapua Magnums had less significantly less kinetic energy, but in some cases could penetrate armoured glass. The craftsmanship shows through with the best sniper rifles, and this is certainly the case with Accuracy International's L115A3 long-range rifle.

The rifle featured an enhanced suppressor, which reduced the flash and noise signature and helped lessen the chances of detection and so helped the shooter survive. An adjustable bi-pod was developed to allow shooters to support the rifle in a set position while locating the target. the L115A3 was not an inexpensive weapon, but the ability to be so accurate remains in a word: priceless and worth the wait, according to Jim, he made the right decision by turning down the MSG90 from Heckler & Koch all those years ago in 1985.

CQB Close Quarter Combat

My own experience, the first time I did CQB live fire training in Germany, being trained by two Special Forces operators one from the SAS and one SBS Jim and I chose the M10 and not the MP 5.

When you look back in time, the MP5 SMG had two attributes that made it the logical choice for hostage rescue CQB work; the first and most important attribute is that it is controllable on full auto at room distance. This is where the submachine gun shines and is exactly how I feel it should be employed. Second, because it is a pistol calibre, over penetration of the target is minimized. This is crucial for hostage rescue work. The last thing you want to do is engage a threat and have it gone thru and hit the person you are trying to save.

But as a primary tool for CQB are its range limitations. The military In addition to having to shoot targets at room distance in the target building, military operators also have to deal with a 360-degree threat of targets out to medium distance as you approach and depart the target area.

Both urban and rural environments if it is a “hot target”, you can expect to have to engage defenders/enemy targets out past 100 meters as you approach the target, before you conduct your CQB mission. This includes all the way thru the mission on target and even when departing the area on “Bug out”. The last thing most Marines want to have to try and do is suppress AK-47 wielding assailants at 200-300 meters with an MP5 submachine gun–which is generally only good for consistent hits out to 100 meters–on both approach and "Bug out".

Weapons like the MP5 are still carried on missions due to their compact size. With the right method of engagement, I feel you can make up for its pistol calibre stopping power by dumping large amounts of rounds into the target area, driving the target down. I prefer the technique of aiming for the chest and walking rounds up towards the head with full-auto burst of fire.

Jim and I used this method in a "Bug out" situation on our course at the LERP School in 1985, the instructor (SAS) asked, "where did you two learn to fire like that"? Jim replied quick as you like "Stanley 82" alluding to the fact that we had both been engaged in a 4-hour fire fight on the 2nd of April 1982 defending the Falkland from an invading Argentinian force of 2000 compared to our 64!

Minutes later we saw a man arrive in a civilian care who looked a little irate and started talking loudly at one of the German instructors in German. After he left, still a little bit angry by the sound of the wheels screeching away, we were asked if any of our rounds went over the top of the 'Butts' which filled with sand, catch the live rounds. I looked over at Jim and he looked at me and we both replied 'No'. During the 'Bug out' I definitely heard a clunk as the breach block on the M10 stayed back as it operates a blowback open bolt action, when I turned the weapon over to take a look, the tilt to the right with my wrist allowed the barrel to tilt upwards towards the sky, and to my horror the bolt was still moving backwards and forwards sending rounds over the top of the 'Butts' and apparently into the fields beyond, landing next to the guy as he worked on his farm, apparently. I quickly dropped the barrel back down and carried on, lessons learned, with short, barrelled weapons the slightest movements alter the rounds trajectory by a lot.

At the start of the CQB course they had us standing in front of full-length mirrors in a classroom pulling pistols from the holster and pointing at the target before firing, and I now see why they drilled us with short barrel discipline your natural response is, you want to shoot at the largest part of the body and put rounds into it until you see a reaction. Aiming at a small target such as a head takes conscious thought. I think it's just as fast and easier to shoot a rapid string centre mass to the torso kill zone area and drive the target down, even on semi-auto.

With a submachine gun such as a MP5 or M10, it's even faster and easier to give a quick burst centre mass. If your primary method is to shoot bursts or strings to the centre chest, it is easier and faster to walk the rounds up from the chest to the head. With a 5-round burst, the target will start feeling rounds thru the base of the neck, neck and head–not to mention if you put rounds through their arms or hands while they are holding a weapon. Our method of engagement would be to send a burst at the pelvic cradle to start collapsing the threat then burst towards the head. Shots to the pelvic area are not instantly incapacitating, but they will start the process of putting your target down and can allow you the time to transition to the head.

Heckler & Koch is one of the world's leading manufacturers of small arms with firmly established roots in Germany. For more than 60 years, the company has been a reliable partner to security forces, the Special Forces. The selection represents the highest of quality, as well as innovative products.

Heckler & Koch is the only supplier of small arms to offer a comprehensive range of products incorporating pistols, machine pistols, assault rifles, precision rifles, machine guns, Let's remember, introduced in the early 1980s, the standard British Army assault rifle is a compact 5.56x45mm NATO gas-operated, rotating bolt bull pup weapon developed and manufactured by Royal Small Arms Factory and BAE Systems. The complete series consists of 4 models the L85 IW Individual Weapon, which was the standard service rifle, L86 LSW, Light Support Weapon, light machine gun, L22A1 Carbine the short carbine version and L98A1. Due to numerous functional problems in tough foreign missions, Heckler & Koch was involved in the conversion and modernization of the SA80 as early as 2001.

COP Close Observation Platoon

In the 1977 Major General Dick Trant introduced the Close Observation Platoon (COP) based in the county of South Armagh, the IRA's main county. The Recce troop procured primary information on a particular area to facilitate the subsequent work of the specialists deployed in rural areas. Commando units were directed to form Close Observation Platoons in May 1977. These were tasked with uniformed covert surveillance. Small, highly specialist units were raised to conduct covert surveillance and to collect HUMINT. By the end of the 1970s one Regular soldier in every eight serving in Northern Ireland was directly involved in intelligence.

Close Observation Platoon are specially selected and trained men from Recce troop. The highlight of the training is when you get to infiltrate several public locations in Dover completely off-radar, and spend a week watching a target point for that ten second exposure. This is reconnaissance in urban environments wearing plain clothes and having to gather Intel and apprehend high value targets. It was decided that all major units deployed to NI would each provide a 'Close Observation Platoon' to augment the surveillance capacity of the Special Forces.

Close observation troops are formed by each major unit in Northern Ireland as part of the expansion of "SAS-type activities "These troops will take over the close observation role hitherto carried out by the NIPG. (Northern Ireland Patrol Group) will thus perform a role which is like but distinct from that of the SAS. Their method of operation will, however, provide the same justification for the issue of the Remington Wingmaster shotgun, but not a 66mm! Their surveillance operations will be carried out from covert Ops and, although they will operate in uniform, they will travel to their area of operations in civilianized cars. This type of training taking place in Ballykinler, which is situated on the southeast coast of Northern Ireland, right on the coast with a blue flag beach overlooked by the Mourne Mountains.

The importance of developing first rate intelligence structures, processes, and capabilities, so that military operations may be intelligence-led, and non-military initiatives carefully planned and directed. Effectiveness will be judged by what can be gathered, and by how well the product is shared and used.

I attended the course as a team member of 45 Cdo Recce troop in Ballykinler 1986, intensive both physically and mentally. Most Instructors were from 14, Int, NISS and other small NI units, the OC was SAS. The physical side of it was quite hard with 5-8 mile runs along the beach on shingle followed by several PT tests like the USMC test. this was every day and it got harder as the days got longer. May wasn't a good time for a COP course as the gorse was in full flower and the grass long especially if you suffered from hay fever.

You can't just ask to go on this course. If your Unit is due to send personnel on it, they will already know about well in advance and be working out who to send. Then they will run
pre course training and select the best personnel available. Selection is common knowledge along with fitness, map reading, drills, and skills Exactly like recce troop standing operational procedures. They still do the stretcher race and log run which are always

interesting. Wonder if the pain frame still exists and if the log runs to the power station are as much fun?

It's not hard to fathom out the work of a C.O.P, most of the troop before it becomes C.O.P is the Recce troop, and after its stint wherever it would be, it reverts to Recce troop again.

So, it's not hard to work out its role, then again, the name does give it away. But do not take the close in C.O.P as gospel, not with the equipment nowadays. Grow your Hair and Sideburns, maybe a cheeky little moustache too, buy a Rab Bubble Jacket, get some 501's on the go and wash them at least a million times before wearing them so you've got that nice fade look going on, also get a pair of walking boots that are not military issue and try and Fuck them up the best you can before slipping into the naughty little number's, just to give you that authentic COP look. Oh yeah and once in COP you must ignore all the bloke's you used to serve with in the Unit Companies, I think that is also somewhere in the joining instruction'.

One night out in Newcastle, not far from the training camp was a small seaside resort town, Jim, Bob, Topsy and me had a run ashore drinking in the bars. Newcastle was fortunate enough to escape the worst of the Troubles and its residents both Catholic and Protestant lived in relative peace with each other though there has been considerable objection to loyalist band parades in the town. Of the people living in Newcastle, 98% are white. 70% belong to or were brought up in the Catholic faith and 24% belong to or were brought up in a Protestant and Other Christian faith. Little did we know that the bars are split by religion, as we drank in one bar things got out of hand and we spilled out into a carpark area surrounded by angry punters wanting a fight. We each carried a personal weapon concealed under the jacked holstered, the Browning HP is a reliable and accurate 9mm handgun. Its UK military designation is L9A1. The Browning has a magazine capacity of 13 rounds, standing outside this bar in a Mexican standoff situation, we knew if we pulled out these weapons, they would also pull out their weapons and it would end up a right shit storm, so we took a beating and made a hasty retreat into the night.

The training instructors were badged men of the Special air service who do not appreciate being called a 'craphat' as I personally found out during a 'log run' when racing against their team I shouted out "Come on we are not going to let these craphats beat us are we?" The Major in charge nearly took my head off with his verbal assault.

The beasting that followed was memorable to this day, the rest of the troop not impressed with my actions but dug in and showed real enthusiasm for the vigorous exercise calling me a 'wanker' and telling me to shut my mouth.

This kind of training was not new to our troop, and we excelled in all the given tasks, one moment stood out for me which I can still picture in my head now. The boss stood on a bank of grass with the troop gathered around him, some sitting others standing at ease. As he started speaking, we could sense the serious tone in his voice "look around lads, remember the faces standing next to you, some of you will not be leaving this country alive."

I glanced over at Topsy and started to grin, he looked away so as not to show his face, but I know he was cracking up, what a stupid statement from the boss, I expected the following to be expressed "We have before us an ordeal of the most grievous kind. We have before us many long months of struggle and of suffering. You ask, what is our job? I can say: It is to wage war, by sea, land and air, with all our might and with all the strength that God can give us; to wage war against a monstrous tyranny, never surpassed in the dark, lamentable catalogue of human crime." This was a famous speech given by Winston Churchill in1940. The man management skills from the top needed honing I thought, but as you will read later his prophesy came true, in a way! Was it divine inspiration?

Bandit country

Situated in one of the six counties of Ulster which make up Northern Ireland, South Armagh is around 192 square miles in area and home to approximately 23,000 people. As defined by both the British Army and the IRA, it is enclosed to the east by the Al motorway, the main Belfast-to-Dublin Road, to the south and west by the border with the Irish Republic and to the north by an imaginary east-west line running through Mount Norris and Keady. The population of South Armagh is overwhelmingly Roman Catholic, almost exclusively so in the land south of the A25 road. It has been in this 120-square-mile southern portion of South Armagh, including the town of Crossmaglen and the villages of Cullyhanna, Forkhill, Drumintee and Jonesborough, that the overwhelming number of Army and RUC casualties has occurred.

The Border with the Irish Republic was a problem at the strategic, operational, and tactical levels. From August 1969 to the later stages of the campaign republican terrorists used the Republic as a safe- haven although, as has been seen, that became less safe as the campaign progressed. The scope of the problem was considerable. In the late 1970s it was considered that PIRA simply could not survive without refuge in the Republic and the Border also offered opportunities for fundraising from smuggling activities. In 1988 ten of the 16 PIRA ASUs operated from South of the Border.

For many people, this name is only associated with that area in recent times but that is far from the truth, that area of South Armagh that borders on Monaghan has been known as Bandit Country for centuries with tales of famous highwaymen. All counties have their famous place names so too they all had famous highwaymen, rapparees or Tories as they were also known. These are names that ring with romance and danger and the stories abound of these dashing heroes' willingly risking life and limb to help the poor and the downtrodden.

One of the most famous of them all and a man who helped earn the Bandit Country title for South Armagh, Count Redmond O'Hanlon, the Irish Scanderbag He gained the increasing support of the population and as his fame and notoriety spread throughout the land tales of his exploits were even recounted in a French Gazette as he became a truly romantic figure. He thumbed his nose at the authorities and continued to attack British troops that were stationed in a series of outposts between the borders of Armagh and Monaghan.

It is said that history repeats itself and Bandit Country can really attest to this as the British army barracks of recent times, that marred much of South Armagh's beautiful scenery can be interpreted as eerie echoes of the military outposts erected in Redmond's time. Folklore records that there was more than a dozen of them thrown up at remote sites throughout the country and from these daily patrols went out to scour the countryside in search of the outlaw but to little avail. All this back in the mid 1600's, eventually shot in his sleep for a 200-pound reward, Redmond's story live on in the Conwall parish church bearing the O'Hanlon Coat of Arms indicating that this could be the final resting place of the outlaw, Count Redmond O'Hanlon "who banked his treasure in the hearts of the people and whose ghost," local folklore claims, "is still seen riding the highways of Armagh and south Monaghan." The tyrant dies and his rule is over; the martyr dies, and his rule begins.

The Border between Northern Ireland and the Republic was no more obvious and clearly defined than, say, that between Nottinghamshire and Derbyshire. In places it ran along streams, hedges, the side, or middle of roads, and in some places even the middle of farmyards.

The British gradually deployed equipment designed to counter the terrorism in Northern Ireland. Most of this was at the high-technological end of the spectrum and focused on achieving improved surveillance and monitoring systems that would allow for the covert observation of suspected and actual terrorists. These systems were rarely made available to the ordinary infantry battalions. In some cases, this was because the kit was held as a brigade asset, for example the use of Gazelle helicopters using thermal imaging, which came into service in Northern Ireland in 1989. However, more usually it was because there was no real need for the 'green army' to use this kind of equipment. With the introduction of police primacy in 1977, surveillance and intelligence gathering were conducted primarily by Special Forces and key units in the RUC Special Branch. Though CCTV was also used as means of watching the population, it did not prove to be a satisfactory substitute for the presence of troops on the street. Prime Minister Margaret Thatcher authorized the investment of a large sum of money in the acquisition of the latest technology to defeat terrorism in Northern Ireland. Thus, the towers constructed on the border with Ireland used enormously powerful cameras that enabled the observation of suspects at a staggering distance. Intelligence used video cameras that could transmit live real-time TV pictures. These live pictures could then be sent via microwave link to intelligence monitoring stations up to 50 miles away. Covert cameras were also used to monitor IRA activity across the border, which removed the need to deploy Special Forces across into the Republic of Ireland, an activity that had caused considerable embarrassment in the past. In one case, 14 Intelligence apparently had one IRA suspect based across the border under observation for two years and provided a live stream of information on the activities of this individual to the Tasking and Coordinating Group (TCG) South, which accelerated decision making. Equally important was the use of infrared, which ensured that the suspect remained under observation 24 hours a day. Microphones were also attached to cameras, and these could pick up conversations taking place at a considerable distance. Close-up surveillance relied on the use of tiny remote-controlled cameras hidden in cars or disguised to look like part of the natural environment. These cameras provided a constant source of information on the activities of an IRA suspect. The massive improvement in surveillance made it unnecessary to deploy manpower on such risky operations and lessened the chance of the operation being discovered. The security services also made extensive use of bugging to obtain information on the IRA's plans. According to one member of the IRA, the use of all this technology made it extremely difficult for the organization to do anything without the British knowing. It effectively brought the IRA to a standstill.

Permanent observation post in the market square, Crossmaglen – the Borucki Sangar named after Private Borucki of the Parachute Regiment, killed by an IED in the square. The OP was always manned to keep eyes on the square and under surveillance 24/7, after it had been used to mount a mortar attack on the nearby Army base.

Crossmaglen is a place of hostility, isolation, and the constant threat of death. Before going out on patrol, troops are briefed that every gorse bush, stone wall or ditch, every cowshed, milk chum or bale of hay could hide a bomb; if a sniper decided to strike, the victim would probably never even hear the crack of the bullet being fired. In the Square in Crossmaglen, site of a thriving market each month and the place where eight Soldiers have met their deaths in the past quarter century, an IRA memorial has been erected. The inscription reads: 'Glory to you all praised and humble heroes who have willingly suffered for your unselfish and passionate love of Irish freedom.'

More than 30 soldiers have been killed by the IRA in south Armagh's rural hub of Crossmaglen since the conflict began in 1969.

On hilltops outside the town, soldiers in army watchtowers equipped with high-tech scopes and listening gear keep an eye on traffic and farmhands moving about the rolling bog land. In the mid-1980s there were two operations to construct the border permanent observation posts; Op CONDOR to build the hilltop OPs in the Forkhill area, known as the High Romeos, and Op ENTIRETY to cover the approaches to Crossmaglen and the low-lying Golf towers.

Fear is pervasive in south Armagh. In July 1986, the bodies of three local men suspected by the IRA of being police informers were dumped on roadsides near Meigh, Northern

Ireland Motorists passing through this village were stopped at gunpoint one recent night but not by police. The armed men were IRA guerrillas, demonstrating who calls the shots after dark in the corner of Northern Ireland called "bandit country. "

Such roadblocks are a regular Irish Republican Army tactic in southern County Armagh, a rural, mostly Roman Catholic area on the border with the Irish Republic. The aim is to intimidate residents and mock Britain's authority. many residents had a good idea of who the IRA men in the area were, but that none would tell the British authorities.

The small village of Culloville two miles south of Crossmaglen is the southernmost settlement in South Armagh, and the southernmost settlement in Northern Ireland on the border with the Republic of Ireland. The village has a population of 400 people or it did at the time in 1986. It lies within the Newry and Mourne District Council area. The Village is located on a busy crossroads, on the main Dundalk to Castle Blaney road. Three of the roads lead to the South, two to county Monaghan and one to county Louth, while the fourth leads north to Crossmaglen. South Armagh and Concession Road is a place where people are often closely related and the Border, and all that is connected to it, is a backdrop to just about everything.

Those living within the North, most of them on or around Concession Road and many clustered around the village of Culloville, were not supposed to cross the Border using the N53, though many did. With their NI vehicle registration plates, they were supposed to use a manned crossing with all the usual customs posts and checks.

In the space of just a few minutes' observation, many vehicles flew in both directions across Ballnacarry's six-arch bridge. the R179, the road that runs due south from Culloville to another small Border crossing, Kingham's Bridge over the Fane, beside derelict 19th-century corn, and flax mill buildings, about 400m from the village crossroads. On this road, the full bureaucracy of Border checks and inspections was applied to travellers.

Vehicle check points and the value of 'snap' or short-term VCPs, conducted at irregular times and places. This was massively expanded in Northern Ireland to reflect greater numbers of civilian vehicles. Snap VCPs were far more likely to capture terrorists and materiel than permanent VCPs. The indirect advantage was that a prolonged program of snap VCPs had the general effect, of deterring and constraining terrorist movement.

PVCPs were also used extensively. Unfortunately, PVCPs, although useful as OPs and to an extent as patrol bases, rapidly became targets for terrorist. Snap VCPs also risked being the target of attack if their location and timing became predictable and if the tactics used were poor. In addition, a snap VCP has a short useful life. After a few cars had passed through it, word would get round, and even innocent traffic would avoid it.

Air Operations mounted from Bessbrook

Gazelle and Lynx were primarily used for airborne reconnaissance, surveillance and limited troop lift. They were fitted with a variety of observation and surveillance devices at various times. This included real-time TV from quite early in the campaign, and eventually real-time colour video.

Manned airborne surveillance made a considerable contribution to the overall intelligence effort, with aircraft tasking's originating from a wide variety of units and the product going to a similarly wide list of users.

The deployment of the Lynx in 1979 enabled much easier movement of small tactical units. The deployment and movement of VCP parties by helicopter had been conducted from the early stages of the campaign. However, the early generation of AAC helicopters were too small and RAF support helicopters were rarely available sufficiently often to make this a significant tactic. Later on Lynxes were armed with door-mounted GPMGs. A pair would fly a patrol large enough and for long enough to conduct snap VCPs over a wide area. These flights, known as 'Eagle Patrols', developed into a significant part of framework operations, particularly in South Armagh. Helicopters transiting through Bessbrook Mill, or forward based there were included in the intelligence picture. Together with SH and given that overt road movement was forbidden in South Armagh for many years, Army Aviation contributed to a genuinely airmobile concept of operations in South Armagh and several other places.

In the early 1980s No 72 Squadron was the largest in the RAF, with 24 aircraft. In addition, routine insertion and extraction of patrols, SH conducted a considerable amount of logistic movement into and out of remote sites. Roulement units deployed to forward locations from RAF Aldergrove or, occasionally, direct from the Mainland by Chinook. Support helicopters also flew many hours of manned airborne surveillance missions. For several years Northern

Ireland was allocated more than half the total of all UK SH flying hours. RN Wessex's and later Sea Kings also flew support missions, but generally with fewer aircraft. At one time Sea Kings were the only aircraft equipped and trained for night operations out of un-reconnoitred sites. They could be used to deploy and recover patrols at night much more flexibly than other aircraft types, and therefore often came on task late in the afternoon or early evening.

Air mobility also enabled a significant tactical development that of 'operations boxes. These were relatively large areas of ground which were saturated with foot patrols, typically delivered by helicopter. Such operations often involved several companies simultaneously. Patrols would conduct an extensive pattern of snap VCPs, rummage searches and framework patrolling. they frequently prompted terrorist activity either in or around the fringes of the box, which would be detected by other agencies. They could be used to disrupt a terrorist operation, cover the deployment of COP patrols, or several other options. Overall, the effect of air, foot and vehicle patrols creates a tactical synergy which is hard to counter.

Beaver and Islander aircraft were used primarily for airborne reconnaissance. They were closely integrated with the Reconnaissance and Intelligence Centre at RAF Aldergrove. It became entirely a routine for a planned search operation to be supported by up-to-date aerial imagery.

Although a number of helicopters were forced down by gunfire or occasionally mortar fire, security forces retained control of the air throughout the campaign. That was due in large part to a continued process of upgrading aircraft and reviewing flying tactics in

response to changes in the threat. After a shooting incident in 1983 helicopters changed to flying either below 50 feet or above 500 feet, notwithstanding the possible threat of SA-7. IR jammers were introduced to Lynx and Puma from 1985.
A further change in deployment patterns was that from forward basing which optimized the speed of reaction of aircraft deployed to centralization at RAF Aldergrove. there were always some aircraft at Aldergrove and some forward, particularly at Bessbrook Mill, which in the late 1986 was reputed to be one of the busiest heliports in the World. Centralization allowed for better use of assets, but was probably only possible once longer-range, longer-duration aircraft and several forward refuelling sites became available.

It's not like we used many choppers during our operations in 1986, our insertions utilized the now famous white van, Surveillance vans were made to look like decorator's vans, with tins and sheets, but made entirely of fiberglass to boost signals and could hide cameras and men. My personal favourite was the widows blocked with the side of a 'Walkers crisps' box to make it look like a shop van, really!

RUC

Due to the continued problem of political agitation and violence, the RUC had the dual role of combating normal crime and armed subversion from the IRA. It was assisted in the latter role by the Ulster Special Constabulary, which acted as a part-time auxiliary police. Due to its dual role the RUC, continued to be an armed force.in the most difficult areas, such as West Belfast and South Armagh, the RUC could not operate without very considerable support. In practice the Army led operations in those areas until the early 1990s, although the form of RUC support developed continuously. Between those two extremes there was a considerable grey area. Tactically this was reflected in the extent to which the Army acted in Rural Patrol accordance with the RUC's wishes. Issues included the extent of RUC input into the patrol program, and whether all patrols had to be accompanied by a policeman.

The escalation of the terrorist campaign in the 1970's and 80's saw the RUC develop in both size and expertise to meet the challenge. A policy of 'police primacy' was adopted from the mid-1970's, under which the responsibility for security lay in the first instance with the police, with army support available only when necessary. The tactics, and expertise developed by the RUC throughout the conflict prevented four out of five planned terrorist attacks. Despite charges of sectarian and partisan policing and collusion with Loyalist groups, the RUC's undoubted success made it a model for effective counterinsurgency policing.

Enniskillen was the training depot for the RUC from 1938 until it was moved to Garnerville in Belfast in February 1986, in the wake of a devastating IRA mortar attack on the Enniskillen depot.

Training was compulsory for all full-time RUC personnel and lasts for 26 weeks with further training on the job. The training incorporates general fitness, instruction on the powers and code of the RUC, basic law, firearms, riot control and communications equipment. There are further, specialized courses available, both at Garnerville and at military establishments in the North and in Britain. These are augmented by courses for more senior personnel at police colleges in Britain and 'high-flyers' are often seconded to British police forces to gain experience before joining a specialized unit like the Special Branch with all their agents and informers along with their battalions of watchers, snoopers and eavesdroppers tied in directly to their storm troopers in the HMSU for special operations and the DMSUs which scour nationalist areas taunting, harassing, brutalizing Republicans and non-Republicans alike in an attempt to coerce our community into subjection.

The SB will of course warrant a separate section but first to explain about the MSUs in more detail. These are, primarily of two types, the Headquarters MSUs based in Ballykelly, Mahon Rd. Portadown and Knock/Lisnasharragh and are linked into SB, having been involved in the shoot-to-kill controversies of 1982 as well as some more recent operations in Counties Down and Tyrone, sometimes along with the SAS, where volunteers on and off active service have been summarily executed. Yet most of their operations are arrest operations.

For an RUC officer, simply staying alive every day was a task that required considerable planning. Its not possible to overstate the enormity of the pressure faced as they went about their various tasks, one RUC officer said he knew they were not alone in their endeavours. Many other frontline RUC stations faced difficulties of the same nature. Every move we made from our secure barracks had to be weighed up. A balance had to be struck between affording the locals a policing service and protecting ourselves from the constant threat of attack."

The job of both the RUC and Royal Marines was direct collection of low-grade intelligence which relies on the eyes and ears of the entire force, not just the efforts of intelligence specialists. Because insurgents and terrorists blend in with the general population, familiarity with what is normal in an area provides the basis for detecting anomalous behaviour that might indicate insurgent activity. Like the community patrolling police officers do, this strategy leverages an individual ability to learn what the baseline activity is in his area of responsibility and then apply his own human processing power to identify activities of concern.

The focus is on moving as quickly as possible from collecting information to acting on it, transitioning from sensor to shooter, to capitalize effectively on all available information. Intelligence in counterterrorism and counterinsurgency sometimes enables successful operations in which terrorist-insurgent plans are disrupted; adversaries are shot, killed, or captured; cells are rolled up and prosecuted in the courts; or logistical bases are captured, and supply lines broken. Examples of such operations can be found throughout the history of the violence in Northern Ireland.

The RUC, DMSUs are exactly what they say, mobile units attached to each Unit. They are given special firearms training and must maintain a level of fitness and general aggression that would be anathema to the whole idea of `policing' anywhere else in the world. They carry automatic rifles and travel in jeep convoys, but at other times they travel in cars, both armoured and unmarked - depending on the nature of the patrol and the area. Their role in Nationalist areas is to patrol in a high state of alertness a quick reaction force (QRF) to stop, harass and brutalize targeted nationalists and republicans and to mount prearranged search and seal operations at the first report of IRA activity. They operate within their designated divisional areas operating an eight-hour shift and divided up into at least three squads some of these working from the different barracks in the division depending on the size and spread of the division. There is at least one DMSU patrol on the streets and roads of their particular division at any one time.

The Special Branch is divided up into 5 sections:E1 Administration E2 Legal section E3 Intelligence section (with three sub-divisions) E3A Intelligence on republican group E3B Intelligence on loyalists E3C Intelligence on left/communist groups E4 Operations (with four sub-divisions) E4A Operational surveillance E4B Technical surveillance E4C/D

Photographic surveillance and expertise E5 Collation

These groupings are based between HQ Knock and E-Department's base at Lisnasharragh, Montgomery Road, East Belfast. They are organized into three regional HQs: Belfast Region, Castlereagh, North Region, Strand Road, Derry, South Region, Gough Barracks, and Armagh

They are controlled at a regional level by a Chief Superintendent and with a Superintendent in each Division. There is a liaison group with Military Intelligence at Divisional level called Special Military Intelligence Unit. It comprises about 30 personnel taken from E-Department and 14th Intelligence. To return to E-Department's sub-divisions: E1: It is responsible for the supply of all E-Department's resources and contact with all other RUC departments. It controls the large pool of unmarked cars, which are maintained to a very high standard. These are known as Q-cars and must be as ordinary as possible, and not show any of the tell-tale signs of special aerials or other communications equipment. They cannot afford to be armour plated but they do offer a measure of protection by the installation of bullet proof panels inside the doors and seats.

E2 Legal section: It maintains a presence in the main interrogation centres of Castlereagh, Gough and Strand Road to provide the main liaison between CID and Special Branch. It updates special branch on how any suspect is bearing up during interrogation and also to provide access to any information which becomes available as a result of interrogation. The special branch does not usually partake in interrogations. They may take control of an interrogation where a suspect is likely to prove particularly helpful; or in an attempt to recruit someone as an or informer.

E2 will also provide special branch members with the necessary support and direction because of special branch personnel having to appear in court. It also has a liaison with the prison security departments who monitor specified individuals in jail and facilitate requests concerning contacts with informers. It provides staff for the preparation of statements to the CID after special branch controlled operations by E4 personnel.

E3: Its role is to compile information and intelligence on republican (and loyalist) activists. Its personnel target individuals for specific periods and follow and monitor all movements, regardless of who is talked to or what buildings are visited. This will be stored away, and cross referenced and maybe worked on at a later date. The point to remember is that a single individual can lead to the exposure of a complete network of members, houses and dumps The idea behind most of their surveillance is based on the principle that if there is no good reason for a suspect to be in an area then they are "up to no good" and should be recorded. Once the necessary intelligence has been gathered and a picture built up the special branch will decide whether they wish to act on it immediately; or they may sit tight and build upon their picture and thus maximize their potential for causing damage to republican structures etc. The key to most RUC operations is 99% good intelligence, and therefore there are relatively few chance encounters - "just ran into a roadblock" or "spotted by a routine patrol" often serve to hide the true basis of arrest.

Both E3 and E4 have access to a wide array of bugging, monitoring, and tracking equipment. On surveillance missions E3 and E4 carry automatic weapons, radio equipment - including panic button and a number of visual aids for long range surveillance. Unlike their counterparts of earlier years, it is not necessary to carry large photo albums and files. Its operations in the main are targeted on specific individuals who would have been previously photographed and even filmed at length. Its techniques have been learned and updated from the experience of 23 years and is augmented by tactics and incidents involving M15 and M16, and Britain's allies in NATO or elsewhere.

E4C and E4D have specific photographic responsibilities which include the scanning of all photos and film of republican events, whether funerals, parades, or demonstrations. Also, they maintain a watch on certain targeted buildings and check everyone coming and going. Much of this is carried out by recording equipment placed on site and viewed later by E4C/D.

E5: Collation section: this group examines and collate all RUC intelligence using what is relevant to update files and computers, making the various departments aware of any changes and attempting to build pictures of areas - listing "main players" and tying them down to specific roles and incidents.

Apart from the already covered intelligence gathering role the Special Branch has some other functions. These are: Guarding government ministers and visiting dignitaries. This used to be solely a SB responsibility but has been augmented by a specifically trained CID unit in recent years,: with the SB handling only the most senior personnel.

The watching of ports and airports along with the assistance of certain technical aids, they can monitor all those coming and going, and note movement of all known or suspected activists. The guarding of embassy buildings and some of the officials Mostly associated with the English police forces.

The SB liaises with MI5. In the Six Counties special branch often fill the role of "field worker" for MI5.The monitoring of aliens and the corresponding passport responsibilities. There was preparation of several lists for potential foreign internees in the event of "war”. Plus there was preparation of legal papers regarding infringements of the Official Secrets Act.

It is sad but in 1986 the RUC lost 12 people, compared to the 23 lost in 1985 the second worst year for casualties.

'Tiocfaidh ar La'

The Irish Republican Army was founded in 1922. After operating for more than 80 years it is arguably the longest-operating terrorist organization in Western Europe. The origin of the IRA has its roots in a deep conflict over the influence and governance from Great Britain.

The IRA has existed for many years and there have been several leaders. In addition, due to several internal conflicts within the IRA caused by different events, the IRA has split into different factions.

The first split happened at the beginning of the period later called The Troubles in 1969 when the IRA split into two factions, the Official IRA (OIRA) and Provisional IRA (PIRA).

While the PIRA continued their armed campaign against the British, the OIRA was opposed to this. The OIRA, being a Marxist-oriented republican organization, wanted to transform the fight into a united class struggle. However, the OIRA declared ceasefire in 1972, making the PIRA de facto the IRA.

Events during the 1980s once again split members of IRA into different factions such as the Real IRA (RIRA) and Continuity IRA (CIRA). RIRA and CIRA were opposed to the IRA´s participation in the peace process.

Key leaders of the IRA at the time were John Kelly, Thomas Murphy, Bobby Sands and John Stevenson. The leaders of the OIRA, you had Sean Garland and the leaders of the RIRA, Michael McKevitt and Colm Murphy.

The IRA refers to its members as volunteers, which are organized into units. These units were organized into companies, the companies into battalions, which could be part of a brigade. The leadership structure at battalion and company level was mainly the same with its own commanding officer, quartermaster, explosives officer and intelligence officer.

In 1977 the IRA reorganized to improve operational security. A parallel system of Active Service Units (ASU) was formed to conduct terrorist operations while the old "companies" were used to police nationalist areas, gather intelligence, and hide weapons. The ASUs weapons were controlled by a quartermaster, who were under direct control of the IRA leadership.

At the top of the IRA leadership, we find the IRA Army Council, which have the authority to conduct day-to-day leadership over operations in addition to directing policy and taking major tactical decisions. Members of the Army Council are selected from the IRA Executive, which in turn are selected by the IRA General Army Conventions (GAC)

IRA´s political wing is Sinn Fein. The political party is strongly associated with the IRA and there are those who believe that members of Sinn Fein have had an active role in the IRA. The main tactics used by the IRA in its military strategy has been bombings, assassinations, and armed assault, in addition to kidnappings, punishment beatings and extortion. They have also conducted smuggling and robberies to raise funds and arms.

Although advance warnings were given in some cases, attacks without prior warnings were also conducted. The IRAs main target in Northern Ireland was the British armed forces, and the police, in addition to attacks against Protestants, both paramilitaries and civilians.

The South Armagh Brigade has pioneered the use of mortars with eight of the 11 new types manufactured since 1974 being first fired by the Crossmaglen IRA unit

Semtex was first used by the IRA in South Armagh and radio-controlled bombs were developed there. Bicycles torches, Irish tricolours and the bodies of informers have all been elaborately booby-trapped with bombs, a tractor was loaded with explosives and a dummy placed in the driver's seat before it was guided by radio control into the village of Belleek. Five years later, a Real IRA member from South Armagh perfected a bomb that could be detonated by calling a mobile phone, now used all around the world by terrorists and insurgents as well as the tribes in Afghanistan and Iraq.

Counterintelligence units tried Reducing Mortars attacks by assessing firing platforms marked by fence posts where vans or small Lorries could pull up and fire the mortars off and drive away un-noticed. With a range of cameras and explosive sensing capabilities to assess the likely presence of explosive devices loaded on Traditional Vehicle Borne (VBIED).

Mortars fired from the back of a tipper truck and with a total weight of 120 lbs. The truck had markers preplaced either side of the road to line up the correct distance from the target these ‘Firing points’ if spotted beforehand became a surveillance point where an OP provided eyes on plus reactive fire power.

PIRA began to claim security force fatalities in the mid-1980s. A series of attacks around this period show PIRA’s growing confidence in the technology and tradecraft necessary to mount successful mortar attack against military bases. In Northern Ireland, attacks against rural targets more prevalent, illustrating both the capabilities and operating freedoms enjoyed by South Armagh Brigade of PIRA along with the suitability of rural targets.

A “Player”, a member of an unlawful organization styling itself the Irish Republican Army, otherwise Óglaigh na hÉireann, otherwise IRA, a powerful South Armagh farmer known as 'the Boss'. the Boss was a senior IRA man who owned a farm and dealt in cars, lived six or seven miles from Dundalk, The Boss had been the central IRA figure in South Armagh for more than 25 years and was also the IRA's Chief of Staff, the leader of the world's most feared paramilitary organization. South Armagh was being watched and revealed that a wealthy pig smuggler' living in the Irish Republic had been responsible for the Killeen attack. The pig smuggler's name was Thomas Murphy. He owned and controlled the Murphy farm complex.

At the height of the British military presence there were 18 watchtowers in south Armagh. One of the key reasons for constructing the posts from 1986 was to watch Thomas Murphy, the then-IRA chief-of-staff whom MI5 once classified as the most dangerous terrorist in Europe. Two of the posts overlooked the millionaire smuggler's farm, which straddles the Irish border.

In 1985 “Slab Murphy” was appointed the Provisional IRA operations commander for Northern Ireland and had sanctioned a planned bombing campaign of 12 seaside resorts in England which was thwarted when British police arrested the IRA active service unit in Glasgow

Murphy (Boss) perfected the use of secondary devices at Narrow Water near Warrenpoint in August 1979 when 11 soldiers were killed in a radio-controlled explosion 32 minutes after seven of their colleagues had perished in the initial blast. Murphy is thought to have orchestrated the operation when armour-plated Ford Cortina carrying four RUC officers was blown apart at Killeen as it escorted a lorry carrying a Brinks Mat gold bullion consignment across the border in May 1985. All four were killed when a 900 lb. radio-controlled bomb packed into an articulated trailer on the hard shoulder was detonated.

'The Surgeon', another notorious commander of the South Armagh Brigade, was among the most trusted volunteers in the IRA's heartland; between them, they had been involved in several hundred attacks on the security forces.

Michael McHugh who shot dead Sgt Patrick Morrissey following an armed robbery at Ardee labour exchange. McHugh, and Noel Callan, formerly of Culloville, Castleblayney, Co Monaghan was convicted of the murder of Sgt Morrissey on 27 June 1985.The officer was initially wounded by McHugh before he shot the unarmed garda in the head.

Current Army Council Circa 1986 Gerry Adams, Martin Mc Guinness, Pat Doherty, Brian Gillen, Tom Murphy, Gerry Kelly, Martin Ferris, back in the day printing these names you could be found in a black bag on the side of the road in South Armagh with a bullet in the head.

All roads lead to Dundalk where most of the IRA players lived like Jerry's brother, Liam Adams who got exiled to Muirhevnamore because he was a tout? People still wonder if people like: Malachy Foots, Kevin Meehan and Briege Elliman live there in Dundalk to this day. PIRA's members Aiden

Moley, Danny McNamee and Donal Moyna still live there apparently!

Brian Arthurs, Derek Brady, Saoirse Breathnach, Alan Brown, Mickey McDonald, Tommy Clare, Seamus Daly, Rauiri Dougan, Patrick Duffy are names mentioned when you ask who still lives over the border. Tommy Eccles, Patrick, McPhillips, and Brian McShane who killed Garda Frank Hand at Drumcree call Dundalk home and Liam Fagan, Niall Farrell, Jim Fox, Eibhlin Glenholme's who may be back in Belfast with Bobby Campbell, Donna Maguire Hardy, Owen Hanratty, Paul Kelly, Sean Kenna, Damien Lawless, Darrin Mulholland, Kieran, and Paddy McDonagh? Is Martin McDonagh a leader nowadays Bic McFarlane still lives there. How about Dalton McKevitt, Vincent McKevitt, Bernadette Sands McKevitt, the list of names goes on and they have not gone away. These people have been mentioned in books written by former high ranking IRA members like Martin Ferris who published his own book which has become the new trend for current IRA leaders who publish books praising themselves for all they have done, but as usual they leave out all the real details we want to know.

Books now available on the involvement are now available by, Jerry Adams are Never Give Up, Falls Memories, Before the Dawn, An Irish Eye, Blackwell Handbook of Adolescence, The New Ireland.

Martin McGuinness the former IRA chief of staff has written books like, A Life Remembered and Before the Dawn, An Autobiography.

One of my fascinations with Northern Ireland in the 1970s and 80s is how it became a place where different rules applied, where reality itself seemed up for grabs. Nowhere was this more the case than the "Provisional Republic" of

South Armagh, AKA Bandit Country, with its handmade “sniper at work” signs and its community militias all surveyed by the watchtowers and helicopters of the British army. Toby Harden’s book is a compulsively fascinating tour of this alternative universe. Aptly named :‘Bandit Country, the IRA & South Armagh’.

In Crossmaglen the still fire burns true, the patriotic flame will never die, And when you hear the battle cry, it will be the fighting men of Crossmaglen, an IRA ballad goes!

OP (Observation Post)

The towers lining the sky line of the beautiful country side were manned by rifle companies as a routine part of operations. They provided several benefits. Firstly, they provided 24-hour weather and largely bullet-proof cover for surveillance operations. Secondly, they allowed the use of more sophisticated surveillance equipment, such as 'Super-Nikon' binoculars and MSTAR radar. Thirdly, they supported the development of an advanced communications network, not least because their hilltop sites typically provided particularly good antenna locations. Fourthly, they allowed for a continuity of observation across wide areas. Sightings of terrorist suspects could be passed from tower to tower over wide areas. The towers had mutually supporting arcs, minimizing problems of dead ground. Sightings were also passed to helicopters operating in the area. Lastly, the towers provided a degree of overwatch for foot patrols. Insertion to the observation posts and conduct the operation will be covert in nature. Overt observation posts like the watch towers will be hardened positions to increase security. A patrol provides cover while the observation post is being inserted. A covert observation post relies on stealth of insertion and occupation for protection. It is normally positioned in abandoned buildings or thick woods to cover sectors of observation that overt observation posts cannot. Because of their nature, covert observation posts are difficult to successfully establish. Orders establishing observation posts must address the method of extraction as well as actions upon compromise or attack.

The deployment of the Cougar net across Northern Ireland from the mid,1980s that first gave most units a robust, reliable, deployable, and secure means of tactical communications. However, the fight to communicate was but one aspect of the electromagnetic struggle. Terrorist organizations were also involved in what was genuinely electronic warfare from early in the campaign, loyalists were found to be jamming the BBC from a UDA club in Belfast in the early 1970s. A Royal Signals electronic warfare team located the jammers using electronic support measures (ESM) equipment. The club was raided, the individuals arrested, and the equipment seized.

RCIEDs presented another challenge. Early IRA IEDs used commercially available model aircraft components. Simple counters could be devised, but manufacturing, fielding, and using the equipment by all the troops at risk were a major operational challenge. The situation rapidly evolved into a continuous struggle between development and counter. The security forces developed policies to manage this process. Initially the response was largely technical based on the four strands of detection, inhibition, initiation, and surveillance. This was developed into a more sophisticated process which linked tactical and technical measures tailored to the threat.

When a new threat was identified the first response was generally the deployment of detectors. As technical counters were found, equipment switched towards the use of inhibitors. Another issue was that wherever possible equipment should be integrated into a single item. This was important both for man-pack and vehicle configurations.

On one occasion a soldier lost a piece of patrol equipment which fell into the hands of the IRA, who analysed it and developed a counter which then killed at least one soldier. That is one reason why the loss of equipment was, and remains, in this type of campaign, a serious issue. The problem was hugely compounded because the unit involved did not report the loss of equipment until the end of its tour. That gave the

IRA a head start, which was more than long enough. We rarely carried the radio during overt operations and never on covert ops as it was too heavy and bulky.

Chance finds of IED components led to other rapid response developments. In the 1980s an IRA device was found and analysed by scientific experts. Within one-week tactics had been adjusted to mitigate the effectiveness of the device. A technical modification to patrol equipment was developed and fielded within a month. The particular device was effectively obsolete within three months: no such device functioned against a patrol again after the countermeasure was fielded.

Our first OP was to observe a farm and record the activities from our position, a position occupied by four fully kitted Royal Marines was a gorse bush the size of a small car. This bush sat at the bottom of an oak tree, from where one of the team spent 2 hours watching in the direction of the farm. At the bottom of the tree sat another team member, who had the task of protecting his mate up the tree. The other two team members of our group either slept, ate or like me, read a book, on this OP I read The Fellowship of the Ring, the first book of the Lord of the Rings series by J.R.R. Tolkien, a book that excels in a number of things. One of these is expertly immersing you in the world of Middle Earth. The author slowly pieces together the world by having characters not explain things to the reader, but instead to other characters. The book does this in a way that allows you to take in all its information easily. Another thing the book does seamlessly is developing characters. For example, Sam is a seemingly underwhelming hobbit. Yet, throughout the book, you can see his courage building and his desire to protect Frodo overpower any thought of his personal safety.

And finally, the book leaves no plot holes. Like when Frodo asks Gandalf why he can't take the ring, the answer is given that the power of the ring is limited to the power of the wielder. Hobbits are low on the food chain, so the ring does not do much in their hands. All these qualities contribute to one of the most beautifully written books of the century that has stood the test of time.

Reading this book in low light and cramped conditions hidden by the cover of the thick gorse bush was a great experience in its own. Our team, Bob, Jim, Topsy and I had just settled into the routine when on day two Jim and I sat inside the bush stood down on time off to eat and sleep, no hot food allowed as the cooking lets off smells which can drift for miles. Jim had made a cold porridge with cold water he put the pot up towards his mouth to slurp the stuff down, when an almighty explosion went off sending shock waves through my entire body and the porridge all over Jim's face. Once I got over the shock and checked myself for any wounds, we both started smiling silently waiting nervously for any news from Bob and Topsy on duty, had they seen anything? What was it? Two minutes later we all sat in a three-foot space huddled together, whispers and relief flooding out from all of us, thankful that we had not been the target. still to this day do not know what happened the explosion could be heard for miles and sounded like a 1000 pounder going off. 09 July 1986 Bertram, Robert , British Army, Killed by Irish Republican Army, Killed by remote controlled bomb hidden in car, detonated when British Army foot patrol passed, Glassdrumman, near Crossmaglen, County Armagh. In the same patrol Carl Davies, British Army,

killed by remote controlled bomb
Five days we stayed on location before moving out and back to Drumadd Barracks military installation in the back of a white van with crisp boxes in the windows for some R&R it was the 12th of July and home for 2nd Battalion, Ulster Defence Regiment, and 2 Para at the time.

'Murphy's gang' were notorious in Northern Ireland. Our Boss a lieutenant in the Royal Marines pointed to the Slab's farm complex on a map and said: "This is where in South Armagh everything stems from." I remember those words like he said them yesterday.

Thomas Murphy had for some years been actively involved in fuel smuggling and other forms of smuggling across the border between the Republic of Ireland and Northern Ireland. The border dissects the original dwelling house and farmyard with most of the dwelling being in Co Louth and approximately just over half of the yard area in Co Armagh.

This farm straddles the border with substantial buildings in both jurisdictions, some of which have the border going through them. It is the convenience of the location which lends itself to the illegal trade of fuel.

In 1986, several million pounds was spent building watchtowers at Drummuckavall and Glasddrumand known to our Recce troop as Golf Two Zero and Golf Three Zero respectively to dominate the area to the north of the Slab Murphy farm complex.

As mentioned earlier Tom Murphy was believed by the RUC and Army to have been involved with the development of IRA mortars in the early 1970s. In March 1979, the IRA claimed its first victim in a mortar attack when Private Peter Woolmore was killed by a direct hit as he relieved himself in the ablutions block' inside Newtown Hamilton security force base. It was the first use of the Mark 10 mortar, made up of 45 lbs. of fertiliser explosives packed into a gas cylinder and set off by a propellant ignited by a photo flash bulb. Mark 10 mortars later killed nine police officers at Corry Square RUC station in Newry in 1985.

Two Sniper ASUs were involved in sniping operations on the boarder and, although there were some long-distance shoots using the Barrett, most engagements were at a range of 200 to 300m using a 7.62mm rifle. The attacks, which were carefully mounted to use dead ground away from the Army's matrix of observation posts targeted security forces on their likely movement routes near bases and vehicle Many of the shots were from the back of a specially converted car which was immediately driven away to avoid leaving any forensic traces.

Mortar firing point OP

Intel had information on a 'mortar firing point' in our area of operations. To prepare a large-scale attack, multiple bombs need to be constructed requiring time, skill and access to a sizable space such as a farm. As attacks move from planning into execution, explosives will either need to be synthesised or moved from weapons hides. Watching premises and vehicle movements, along with covert source, policing intelligence yield important clues about impending attack. Acquisition of explosives, precursor materials and detonators are critical steps for the terrorists, our Training in detection of hostile surveillance, suspicious activity such as a dry run and vehicles in the area.

We inserted from Armagh city in a civilian van disguised as a shop van, every civilian in the area knows who uses theses van's, they are not very covert. Once in the position from which we had "eyes on" our four-man team 'Two One Charlie' settled into an 'OP' routine of camouflage and concealment.

The Royal Marines demand high standards of personal cleanliness. Even in the field, Royal Marines are required to wash themselves thoroughly and in camp a high standard of cleanliness is demanded. There is little doubt that some of the concern with cleanliness has become a means of distinguishing themselves from other combat arms in the Army. Cleanliness has become a status marker for the Royal Marines. the standards of cleanliness in the Royal Marines are derived from the Royal Navy, whose concerns for hygiene on board ship are well known. Cleanliness is not just a status marker, however, separating the Royal Marines from the Army. It is operationally important.

Royal Marines concern with personal cleanliness is related to operational effectiveness. On commando operations, it is essential that all ranks can be trusted to look after themselves and their own equipment. This is ingrained into your very core from basic training, field craft lesson one.

When preparing for insertion into the OP, no deodorants to be used at least a week before and not to be packed in the kit needed for the operation. Other items not allowed are toothpaste, shaving foam scented soaps, and cigarettes all of which could give away the position.

A dead letter box, dead drop, is used to exchange our rubbish like shit bags and any reports for int. ('drops') with a covert contact without having to meet them, contact them or use an intermediary. We can leave a package without a risk of it being discovered or accidentally disturbed. We would use a knot in a tree trunk or a gap between a wall and hedgerow. A live drop would involve a van or car pulling over next to a pre-planned location with the window down so we could throw the rubbish bag into the rear and the driver would throw out food and any other requested equipment onto the floor for collection and drive off.

As a four-man team we carried various weapons for the job, personally carrying the US-made M16 with attached M204 grenade launchers, and a 'Glock 17' hand pistol it had the perfect balance for a 9mm. The barrel length gives good stability, accuracy, and concealment, while the grip is just right for pretty much any hand size. The angle of the grip and the stippling also aided in recoil control The Glock 17 was at the time about as good as a 9mm could get.

Jim preferred the Remington 870. A manual, pump action shotgun, the "870" for close range protection from within the 'OP' along with a regular The M16 rifle, Calibre 5.56 mm, M16, is a family of military rifles adapted from the ArmaLite AR-15 rifle. Or more commonly known, the M16A2.

Note back in 1986 when only a SAS patrol could carry a lightweight rocket launcher in order to deal with armoured threats. The LAW 66mm is a one-shot disposable rocket launcher that is highly effective against soft skinned vehicles and light armour, up to a range of 200 meters.

Three days into the 'OP' we received a message via a dead letter box that a SAS team had been tasked to take over the observation post armed with 66mm and we had to handover the 'OP' at 02:00 hours we could smell the SAS boys before we heard them moving close to our position.

We had left the position clean, no gash, the only sign we had been there was the flattened ground inside the gorse bush. When Bob had completed the handover, which took about two minutes we moved of back towards Glassdrumman to await further orders.

Inside the Glassdrumman tower complex we slept underground in bunkers when not on watch in the OP tower. We expected to see or hear the SAS take out the mortar team soonest, but nothing for two days, when they either got 'Intel' or board! And asked our team to move back into the OP and take over the operation without the 66mm of course.

One of the lads 'Stan the man' had a plan, God knows where he got the grey plastic pipe from, but he cut a length 0.775 m long and painted the thing green and grey and camouflaged it with great care , so it looked something like a M72 LAW which the

SAS guy had carried into our position a couple of days before hand. We set off in the dead of night arriving on location at 03:00 hours. As we approached the 'OP' we could see the SAS boys sitting around outside the bush giving protection to our team as we made our way inside our old position, 'Stan' had the water pipe held in the crook of his left arm with his M16 on his right side.

One of the SAS boys whispered, "What's that mate?" to Stan as he entered the bush, his reply was 'Class' he relied in a whisper "sorry mate can't tell you that, if I told you I would have to kill you!" I nearly pissed myself struggling to keep my laugh inside.

They had been in the position for less than 48 hours and the smell of piss and shit was difficult to ignore, gash (empty ration packs and packets of used food) lay everywhere with small bags crammed into every little nook and cranny of the gorse bush structure. They had left everything apart from the 66mm, field craft left a lot to be desired, suppose that's why they call them 'Pongos' where the Army goes the pong goes!

We organized and cleaned the position and settled into our routine once more. Three more days and 'Intel' pulled the plug, it was obviously not going to happen, had all the movement been spotted? In any case we got out and back to base for a hot shower and some clean clothes for a day of drinking which was not a good idea as it happens.

Culloville House on concession road

While inside the Glassdrumman tower complex, our team received orders to carry out an odd ball, recce on a bar in the small town of Culloville. The plan was Topsy and I would move off the hill and down into the village under the cover of darkness and get as close as possible to the pub on concession road. As 'close as possible' was up to the window and look inside.

Much of the motivation of the terrorist came through a wish to glamorize a somewhat third-rate way of life, through esteem amongst the republican community or, more simply, in bars or with women. Denying terrorists, the opportunity to commit terrorist activities will tend to undermine that aspect of motivation.

A player named John Tonra drank in the bar and 'Intel' wanted eyes on him and his female accomplice on a certain date. While getting our brief from our boss on how we planned to insert and extract without being seen or heard a thought entered my head which scarred me to death.

My Mother had left my father when I was aged 13 years old to live with an Irish man named 'John Tonra' I knew she moved over to Ireland and stayed in Cork, but was this the same John Tonra? As Topsy and I made our way through the small hedgerow surrounded fields on route to the bar, all I could think about was looking into the bar and seeing my own mother sitting there with an IRA player in a bar watched by the security forces.

My head was not in a real good place as we stealthily moved forward attempting to make good progress down the hill, now one basic rule is accepted while moving about rural South Armagh and that is never use gaps in the hedgerows to enter the next field as it may be booby trapped with explosives. Time was getting on and we needed to get 'eyes on' before the bar closed at midnight and we still had around 200 m left to go, Topsy and me could not find a way through the thick hedge surrounding the last field. There was only a gap two foot wide right at one end of the field in the corner. It looked like a prime booby trap position and was screaming out, 'Don't walk through here'!

Turning around to whisper in Topsy's ear "Stand back" and as he took a few paces back I put my fingers in my ears and used one of the best-known sketches from Monty Python's Flying Circus which features John Cleese as a bowler-hatted bureaucrat working with the fictional, Ministry of Silly Walks. It's a classic physical comedy. Out of frustration and fatigue I decided to just walk through the space and step into the gap, I actually had the London tube station warning running through my mind at the time 'Mind the gap' and moved forward by slapping my booted foot on the ground, fully expecting to feel shockwaves and maybe hear the

IED explode or at least feel pain as my leg was lost and turned me into a heap screaming 'Medic' with life-threatening injuries, a severely injured left arm and a badly mangled right leg. I would remember everything from the time of the explosion to the time of the yellow and orange heat in my face, to the time the tremendous jolt to my right leg, maybe seeing my leg gone or seeing my arm turned 180 degrees I might even have seen that my femoral artery had been cut, but thank the Lord!

Nothing! That simple act of stupidity saved an hour and the chance to complete our task, Topsy was fuming. After around 30 minutes we had positioned ourselves under one window with our backs along the wall, hoping no one had seen our move, we know one dog had because it was barking for what seemed like an age, luckily no humans took notice of the dog.

My heart was in my mouth as I popped my head up over the windowsill for a quick look into the 'smoke filled room', fully expecting to see my own Mother sitting there laughing and having fun inside. To my surprise the inside of the bar looked void of women, just men drinking around the bar, thick smoke made the room difficult to pick out the features, my quick glimpse saw no faces from my face book so back down below the window, two seconds tops, my exposure not seen. Topsy had another look just to confirm that John was not in the bar. we moved off into the darkness with that dog still barking its head off and made our way back using the very same route we had used earlier, another thing you should never do. When planning a primary and alternate route you should use them. We had selected primary and alternate routes to and from the objective but we broke the cardinal rule.

We had planned and prepared for the recce using the procedures, identify required actions on the objective and planned backwards to departure from friendly lines on the hill, 'Gulf one zero' and forward to re-entry of friendly lines. Because we act independently, and moved beyond the direct-fire support of the resident unit occupying the watch tower observation post, and operate forward of friendly units, coordination was thorough and detailed. Coordination is continuous throughout planning and preparation. We used checklists to preclude omitting any items vital to the accomplishment of the mission. Avoid Detection by the Enemy: we must not let the enemy know that it is in the objective area. If the enemy knows he is being observed, he may move, change his plans, or increase his security measures. Methods of avoiding detection were to minimize movement in the objective area. Move no closer to the enemy than necessary. If possible, use long range surveillance devices or night observation devices. Camouflage, stealth, noise, and light discipline. We used the stealth and camouflage well, but that dog may have let people know we had been there!

On our way back as we got close to the tower we expected a challenge asking for a password especially as we were forward of friendly lines when returning, we had a password but did not need to use as the guy on sentry must have been asleep or away making a cup of tea as we just walked back in unchallenged.

To this day 40 odd years later I still have that image of my mother sitting next to an IRA player in a smoke filled bar laughing at the situation as she spots her Son peeping over the top of the window sill, with his blacked out face showing the shock.

Glorious 12th

After 5 days in the OP gaining very little information on the target we made our extraction via the small roads surrounding the watch towers , we got back to Drumadd barracks on the 12th of July 1986, little did I know, just in time to celebrates the victory of Protestant William of Orange over Catholic King James at the Battle of the Boyne in 1690 with a few lads from the RUC drinking copious amounts of homemade Poitin. Poitin is the Irish whiskey or moonshine which still has something of a mythical status in Ireland, with plenty of rural people able to point to their own source of the stuff, probably outside of any kind of official production. There are numerous stories doing the rounds about as a team we had no sleep to talk of for the 5 days on the operational observation task, so starting drinking moonshine at midday was not the smartest thing to do. The 90% proof has been known to cause serious health issues for those who consume it. Inside the accommodation block we occupied , one of the communal rooms had been set up like a concert room for one of the lads called Billy an Irish boy himself sat in the middle of the room surrounded by a few upside down litter bins made from tin.

He was frantically drumming the bins and singing: “In 19 hundred and 16, the forces of the Crown Did take the orange, white, and green bombarded Dublin town But in '21, Britannia's sons were forced to earn their pay And the black and tans like lightning ran from the rifles of the I.R.A. They burned their way through Munster and laid Leinster on the rack In Connaught and in Ulster marched the men of brown and black they shot down wives and children in their own heroic way and the black and tans like lightning ran from the rifles of the I.R.A. They hanged young Kevin Barry high, a lad of eighteen years Cork city's flames lit up the sky but our brave boys knew no fear The Cork Brigade with hand grenades in ambush waiting lay And the black and tans like lightning ran from the rifles of the I.R.A. The tans were caught, taken out and shot by the brave and valiant few Sean Treacy, Denny Lacey, and Tom Barry's gallant crew Though we're not free yet, we won't forget until our dying day How the black and tans like lightning ran from the rifles of the I.R.A" which had me in tears of laughter especially as we had just finished drinking with the RUC.

We all joined in singing the rebel songs accompanied on drums by Billy, my only contribution was parts of 'Boys of the Old Brigade.'

"Where are the lads who stood with me.

When history was made?
Oh, gra machreee I long to see.
The boys of the old Brigade.
"Oh father, why are you so sad,
on this bright Easter morn?
When Irishmen are proud and glad
Of the land where they were born."
"Oh, son, I see in mem'ries view.
A far-off distant day,
When, being just a boy like you,
I joined the I.R.A
In hills and farms the call to arms
Was heard by one and all,
And from the glens came brave young men
To answer Ireland's call.
'Twas long ago we faced the foe,
The old brigade and me,
But by my side my God and I

So Ireland might be free.

And now, my boy, I've told you why

On Easter morn I sigh

For I recall my comrades all

From dark old days gone by,

I think of men who fought in vain with rifle and grenade

May Heaven keep the men who sleep from the ranks of the old brigade".

Once the room had been destroyed, we moved on, a disco started in the NAFFI around about seven o'clock that night which turned into a personal dance floor for me and Jim and the rest of the team who danced to Simple minds (Don't forget about me). Around ten o'clock a girl band came on and sang a few songs by this time the whole team had started to look and feel a little worse for the weather but continued to drink.

The girls told us they were now moving on to the officer's mess to entertain the officers of 2 Para, RUC and all asunder who used the mess within Drummad barracks at the time. I cannot remember who had the idea to carry on the night and follow the girls into the mess, but three of us did, ending up standing at the bar in the officer's mess. I stood alone at the bar with long unkempt hair waiting to be served a small man came up to me and asked who I was and which unit we belonged to. I stood out like a sore thumb, and in my drunken stupor replied "I cannot tell you that Sir. "To which he replied, and I swear he said, "you can tell me I'm the CO of 2 Para" Being drunk I carried on with the story and he left, a couple of minutes later a man mountain walked over towards me and demanded to know who I was, and why was I drinking in the officers mess? Now things go a little dark as I cannot remember very much about the resulting fight out thru the fire doors and onto a grassy area to the rear of the mess and ending with me running away into the night like a small child shouting childish taunting comments.

The Irish have a name specific to a Poitin hangover, poit, and the stories regarding people going blind after drinking the stuff I can well believe as the next day when I could hear someone shouting, "John get some kit on you have to see the boss asap" See the boss I couldn't see anything for about a minute and my head was splitting in two.

"Get a uniform on and get up to the office now John" I only had a set of 'Jungle lightweights and my green beret' to wear so frantically tried to look presentable for the boss. Once in front of him I saluted and asked what he wanted? "Can you remember what you did last night" he asked me and then told me to report to the Second in command ‘2IC’ of 2 Para ASAP! Locating the Head office for the Parachute regiment wasn’t hard, trying to recollect and sober up was an issue as we stood outside an office waiting for our bollicking, Jim asked me what happened, Bob said he was caught upstairs for some reason in the officer’s mess and did not see my altercation with the guy behind the door. As we marched into his office, we could see a massive man wearing his maroon beret sat behind his desk staring at a sorry sight of three Royal Marines scruffily dressed and still drunk from the poitin.

He introduced himself, then looked directly at me standing to attention in front of him and shouted and pointed his finger towards me “You, you cunt outside now” to which I replied “Sorry sir, I cannot fight with my Green beret on” He then took off his maroon beret and threw it down on the desk and blasted “outside now” and stood up, he was massive, there was no way I was going to fight this guy, not today and definitely not in this state.

The punishment for our drunken escapade was not a fine or military prison; no we got kicked out of Recce troop which hurt more. The next day the three of us got in a car and drove north towards Belfast, we had been sent back to our parent unit 45 CDO who were operating in ‘West Belfast’ as the ‘Emergency Roulement Unit.’

There were further periods of violence following the Orange Order 'Twelfth' parades. Later the Royal Ulster Constabulary released figures that showed there had been 128 RUC officers and 66 civilians injured and 127 arrests made. 281 plastic baton rounds had been fired and there were 79 reported cases of intimidation. Brian Leonard, a Catholic civilian, died two days after been shot while working on a building site in Shugville Street, Shankhill, Belfast. The Protestant Action Force (PAF) claimed responsibility for the killing. The PAF killed two more Catholic civilians during July 1986 and two in September 1986.

I guess, like many who spent time in the place, I remember the beautiful countryside and would go back for that alone. But it would also be interesting to go poking around old haunts. I know Vietnamese battlefields have been a popular destination for US veterans and they have been welcomed by their former enemies. How would a Royal Marine reunion tour of Bandit Country go down with the locals. Well as South Armagh is still the beating heart of the PIRA, I should imagine that you'll be as welcome as shit in your handbag. They haven't gone away you know.
Changers are good and as It was once among Northern Ireland's most

impenetrable landscapes, dominated by razor wire and Army Sangers. More than a decade after the watchtowers were dismantled and troops re-deployed, almost £1 million was to be spent opening up to tourism, the area dubbed 'Bandit Country' during the Troubles.

West Belfast July-Nov 1986

Belfast from Irish: Béal Feirste, meaning "mouth of the sand-bank ford", is the capital and largest city of Northern Ireland, standing on the banks of the River Lagan on the east coast. It is the 12th-largest city in the United Kingdom and the second largest on the island of Ireland. Belfast suffered greatly in the Troubles: in the

1970s and 1980s it was one of the world's most dangerous cities. By the early 19th century, Belfast became a major port. It played an important role in the Industrial Revolution in Ireland, briefly becoming the biggest linen-producer in the world, earning it the nickname "Linenopolis". By the time it was granted city status in 1888, it was a major centre of Irish linen production, tobacco-processing, and rope making. Shipbuilding was also a key industry; the Harland and Wolff shipyard, which built the RMS Titanic, was the world's largest shipyard. Belfast as of 2019 has a major aerospace and missiles industry. Industrialization, and the inward migration it brought, made Belfast Northern Ireland's biggest city and it became the de facto capital of Northern Ireland following the partition of Ireland in 1922. Its status as a global industrial centre ended in the decades after the Second World War. Belfast is still a port with commercial and industrial docks, including the Harland and Wolff shipyard, dominating the Belfast Lough shoreline.

45 Commando Royal Marines performed the role of the Belfast Roulement Battalion from 2nd July to 10th November 1986 with foot patrol setting out from Springfield Road RUC Station daily.

The RUC Station at Springfield Road was 45 Commando's Tactical HQ. With its fortress-like protective fencing it stood cheek-by-jowl among little terraced houses. Marines escorted the constables of the Royal Ulster Constabulary (RUC) on their beat, both on foot and in Land Rovers. A sign warned: Do Not Stand Around in This Yard. Holes made by bullets and shrapnel from bombs tossed over the fence explained the reason why. Our new home with 'X-Company was North Howard Street barracks, an old factory transformed into a military base when the Troubles started. Conditions were cramped and frugal. There was also the constant danger of IRA sniper, grenade, mortar, and bomb attacks on the building. Talk about 'RDP' Rapid deployment one minute I'm sneaking about trying not to be seen next, I'm on the streets in full view waiting to catch a bullet. Tasks given to our unit patrols range from covert surveillance to search operations, foot and vehicle escorts to RUC patrols, clearance operations and vehicle checks. Much of this activity intentionally brings Royal Marines in to contact with the public. When deployed on operations, A Roulement Battalion Marine will spend 41% of his time on patrol tasks. The proportion of that effort carried out at night (that is, away from his bed) is less relevant since he is fully available for duty throughout his tour and apart from four days leave in back home on the mainland , he has extraordinarily little time for recreation. We work a 16 to 18-hour day everyday seven days a week for 3 months before getting a long weekend R&R off back in England or Scotland, Wales.

Although a patrol may be accompanied by Police, the operational circumstances may be such that most Marines on the patrol are not generally in sight of the RUC officers. This occurs in urban areas, West Belfast, where one four-man team (a brick) provides close protection to two RUC officers - but up to five more four-man teams provide essential protection in depth for the "Primary" team containing the police officers. On top of that, two more teams may be mounted in vehicles providing a mobile reserve for the patrol commander. Thus, out of a total Marine force within the patrol of 48 men, only four are in visual contact with the police officers all the time. What the public may perceive to be "an unaccompanied patrol" will in fact be flanking elements of a larger, accompanied, force. These patrols I quickly realised were nothing more than letting paid thugs onto the streets of West Belfast to harass and bully the locals at the slightest sign of any insurrection.

August 1986 The Irish Republican Army (IRA) issued a warning that contractors who were carrying out work for the security services in Northern Ireland would be considered 'part of the war machine' and should be 'treated as collaborators.' This affected a lot of local businesses who supplied services to the security forces.

Certain types of military patrols require a degree of agility of movement and a use of ground that would be inappropriate for a uniformed police officer to adopt. For example, a military patrol of four four-man teams may be tasked to conduct a sweep of an urban area to disrupt a possible command wire Bomb attack. This patrol would move ahead of an accompanied patrol and would move very rapidly using alleys, minor streets and crossing fences at unexpected places. Such a style of movement would be out of keeping with the image required of a Police Officer on the beat.

The bottom line of the British security operation in Northern Ireland was provided by young soldiers who carried an enormous burden of responsibility upon their shoulders.

We are ordered into the streets of Belfast with a weapon in our hands, live rounds in our pouches, enormous powers at our disposal, and then told to deal with normal British subjects. The Marine has been trained as a Marine, how to observe, how to seek out a target and how to shoot.

Suddenly thrown into a situation where he must make the terrible decision between being polite and firm at one moment and shooting to kill in self-defence at another.

We are put through tremendous demands on our personal endurance, resulting from the long hours and the peculiar strains and pressures in this situation. At the same time, we must show almost superhuman patience and self-restraint when patrolling and attempting to help a community that appears only to be antagonized by our presence. I recall how pissed off I was after being spat upon. That was the greatest shock, just being spat on, by an extremely pretty girl. If you're being shot at, it's detached … there's no personal contact. But if someone spits at you it's hate, pure hate. Hatred for British security forces sometimes translated into support for the IRA, both tacit and active. As a classified

British military intelligence report of the time noted, there were plenty of areas where the terrorists can base themselves with little risk of betrayal and can count on active support in an emergency. Nor was there ever a shortage of high-calibre recruits. Gerry Adams wrote that "it is obvious that the IRA exists and operates with the active consent of a sufficient number of people to finance, arm, clothe, feed, accommodate and transport IRA volunteers".

September 14th 1986, while on patrol we intercepted Jim McKernan who was on an IRA mission, where conflicting statements from the government and IRA sources followed the shooting. Eye-witnesses said McKernan had his hands in the air, giving up when he was shot! and could have been arrested. At the inquest which followed the jury accepted the military version of events.

The British military and the RUC had concluded that the main problem they faced was identifying the enemy, so an extensive dossier existed for every person of interest. As a consequence of the security force apparatus and presence required for these operations, nationalist areas of west Belfast began to resemble open prisons.

A couple of years later in 1988, I sat with my Father watching the TV as the killing of two Royal Signals corporals took place live.The soldiers were shot dead after being dragged from their car, stripped and beaten by a mob when they strayed into the funeral cortege for IRA man Kevin Brady, had been mistakenly identified as belonging to the SAS. The two corporals who had the misfortune to end up amid an angry republican crowd were wrongly believed to be members of the Special Forces unit.

The Two Corporals were pulled from their car and executed by the IRA" Belfast March 19th 1988 Executed in cold blood.

The episode is remembered by many as one of the most shocking fatal incidents of the troubles, largely because of the graphic television coverage which showed dozens of men attacking their car. After being taken from their car and beaten, the corporals were driven to waste ground and shot. The incident, which became known as 'the corporals' killings' was seen as both extraordinarily brutal. The sequence of events was watched by an army surveillance helicopter on film which was later produced in evidence at a series of trials related to the incident. The film included harrowing footage of the actual deaths of the soldiers as they were shot by I.R.A. gunmen. The soldiers were pulled from the car as they were blocked from getting out of the area by black taxis. They were pulled out though the windows by republicans, beaten and stripped naked on waste ground before being executed. Although the army version of events was that the soldiers were technicians who were engaged in routine communications and radio work at bases in West Belfast, local suspicions persist that they were instead involved in some form of undercover surveillance activity. Neither explanation, however, is seen as clearing up the mystery of how they came to drive into an I.R.A. funeral attended by many hundreds of republican sympathizers. The incident had its origins in the shootings of three I.R.A. members, by the S.A.S. in Gibraltar. Their funerals in Milltown Cemetery were disrupted by an attack mounted by U.D.A. gunman Michael Stone, who killed three people including I.R.A. member MacBradaigh.

The MacBradaigh funeral was making its way along the Andersonstown Road towards Milltown cemetery when the silver Volkswagen Passat car containing the two corporals appeared. The car headed straight towards the front of the funeral, which was headed by a number of black taxis. It drove past a Sinn Fein steward who signalled it to turn. The car then mounted a pavement, scattering mourners and turning into a small side road. On finding that this road was blocked, it then reversed at speed, ending up within the funeral cortege. When the driver attempted to extricate the car from the cortege his exit route was blocked by a black taxi. At this point most of the mourners and the accompanying republican stewards assumed the car contained loyalist gunmen intent on staging another Michael Stone style attack. Dozens of them rushed forward, kicking the car and attempting to open its doors.

The soldiers inside the car were both armed with Browning automatic pistols and Corporal Wood climbed part of the way out of a window, firing a shot in the air which briefly scattered the crowd. The television pictures showed the crowd surging back, however, some of them attacking the vehicle with a wheel-brace and a stepladder snatched from a photographer. The corporals were eventually pulled from the car and punched and kicked to the ground. They were then dragged into the nearby Casement Park sports ground where they were again beaten, stripped to their underpants and socks and searched. According to republicans, an identification card which read 'Herford', a location in Germany, was mistaken for 'Hereford', the headquarters of the S.A.S… It appears this was important in sealing the fate of the soldiers. With the I.R.A. by now involved the corporals were further beaten and thrown over a high wall to be put into a waiting black taxi. It was driven off at speed, camera crews capturing its driver waving his fist in the air.

The corporals were driven less than 200 yards to waste ground near Penny Lane, just off the main Andersonstown Road. There they were shot several times. Corporal Wood was shot six times, twice in the head and four times in the chest. He was also stabbed four times in the back of the neck and had multiple injuries to other parts of his body. The priest Father Alec Reid arrived on the scene. One of the most enduring pictures of the troubles shows him kneeling beside the almost naked bodies of the soldiers, his face distraught as he administered the last rites. The events of March 19, 1988, lasted only 15 minutes but, because of the nature of the deaths and because much of the sequence was televised within hours, they are regarded among the most shocking in Northern Ireland's recent history.

Later in the day the I.R.A. issued a statement. It said 'The Belfast Brigade, IRA, claims responsibility for the execution in Andersonstown this afternoon of two SAS members, who launched an attack on the funeral cortege of our comrade volunteer Kevin Brady.

Dad turned to me and asked why the guys didn't open up when they had a chance? I had no answer for him, but suspect the use of the 'Yellow card' affected their actions that day, as the new guys on the block, who got lost during a familiarisation of the area, they feared the repercussions of opening fire and killing civilians on live TV.

Crumlin Road Gaol OP

The 640 cell Victorian Crumlin Road Gaol was built between 1843 and 1845; its wings are three stories high at one part of the building and four stories high at another. The building is surrounded by a high five-sided wall. Crumlin Road Gaol stands in the middle of what was once a hotspot of violence where police and army struggled to contain bloodshed caused by bombs and gun battles.

The predominantly Protestant Shankhill Road is just yards away from the prison, and a short distance again from the predominantly Catholic Falls Road

The prison served mainly as a remand prison for suspected terrorists/paramilitaries from both the Republican and the Loyalist sides, who were, naturally, kept segregated.

During the 1970s the prison was often overcrowded with up to three prisoners per cell. Informally the prison is known as "The Crum".

One of my first tasks after joining X-Coy was manning an observation post from within the jail which looked down onto a terribly busy junction on the Shankhill road, the small stone room at the top of a watch tower had a slit to view the outside world happening in real time as normal people went about their daily lives. I sat down and started reading my book by the light coming through the small opening sitting as close as possible to the small cast iron radiator fixed to the wall which was absolutely covered in spit and sperm from countless wanks that had happened in the dark secluded position, it really was disgusting inside that primitive tower.

Reading books was the best way to while away the long hours of watch in the Observation post and I can personally remember every 'OP', by what book I read while on watch and in position monitoring any abnormal movements by the locals.

The Crumlin Road Gaol 'OP' was Tinker, Taylor, soldier Spy by John le Carré who in real life served in MI6 in Germany; he knows what he is writing about. And MI6 (aka SIS or the Special Intelligence Service) in his time was tortured by the search for "moles". The "diplomats" Guy Burgess and Donald Maclean had already fled to Moscow. But the full depth of Soviet penetration into British intelligence – the identities of the Cambridge Five (the other three were Kim Philby, Anthony Blunt, and John Cairncross), recruited as double agents before the war, and the damage they had done – was only beginning to become clear in the early 1960s.

It's often said that spying is a force for peace; the more you know about your adversary and his plans, the less likely he is to take you by surprise and usually the less reason you have to fear him, was that me all those years ago?

Four hours is a long time to keep concentrated especially when you have no interest in the situation but the building up of low-grade intelligence is particularly important against groups like the IRA that adopt decentralized structures for security purposes. British security forces were quite successful in decimating a number of other terrorist the ability of British security forces to turn any members of the centralized groups made possible the identification of entire geographic units. This low-grade intelligence came from people like me, a direct collector with the eyes and ears watching the insurgents and terrorists blend in with the general population looking for anomalous behaviour that might indicate insurgent activity. Observing the interactions down on the streets, hoping to spot a face of insurgent suspects whose positions and activities were of particular interest, increased the intelligence gathered.

Even if it was possible to harness the eyes and ears of every Marine out on patrols and observation post there was always areas that we could not access, so as the counterinsurgents we had to rely on the other eyes and ears, the public as they go about their daily business they observe actions and overhear information of immeasurable value to the security forces.

While British security services deployed a range of intelligence efforts that relied on direct observation and information collected by individuals, such operations always had inherent risks. Therefore, technical tools were needed to provide alternative and complementary ways to gather information. Such tools were also important force multipliers because there frequently weren't enough specialized surveillance operatives to satisfy the demand for their services

Strategies applied in Northern Ireland included such traditional means as airborne sensors with live feed television, sophisticated photographic devices, and infrared detection systems. Listening devices, phone taps, hidden cameras, motion detectors, and technologies that intercepted communications traffic also played a critical role.

The critical task of identifying and tracking IRA activities meant that photographic surveillance approaches were applied in ways more akin to how they would be used by law-enforcement agencies than in traditional military intelligence gathering.

Photographing terrorist suspects and using them to identify their associates was vital to building dossiers and identifying people who might be recruited as agents. When we identified sites, such as arms caches, residences, or commercial buildings that terrorist group members used, security forces frequently chose to monitor the sites with audio and video surveillance for extended periods to identify unknown terrorists or supporters.

The job of weaving this low-grade intelligence data together into a coherent picture lay with people initially, data management, banks of card files and lists of photographs of potential PIRA members or sympathizers. We had Face books with us while observing the public trying to match real faces with photos, with little effect.

As the counterinsurgency continued, these tools evolved into complex databases and computerized information management systems. Descriptions of intelligence efforts indicate that there were individual systems for data on vehicles (code named Vengeful) and individuals (code named Crucible).

Critically, data was collated from across the collection spectrum. Law-enforcement organizations, for instance, fed their intelligence into a unified criminal intelligence system: Monitoring of terrorist suspects and their supporters was also carried out and the details forwarded to an intelligence-collating facility. These details would be entered into a computer system (Not in my day!), where an easy and retrievable reference could be made, and a composite print out of the date, time, and place of the sighting of the vehicle could be accessed.

Every single piece of information reaching the RUC from any source was systematically collated. The ballistic and forensic reports on every incident were married with even the most inconsequential scraps of intelligence.

The Increasingly effective linkage of security activities, into the overall political conflict had drastic reductions in PIRA's freedom of action and effectiveness. In one of the highest compliments a combatant can pay, Brendan Hughes said that intelligence efforts had effectively brought the IRA to a standstill where it could move very little. Brendan Hughes, known locally as 'the Dark' due to his swarthy complexion, is an iconic figure for contemporary Irish Republicans. In particular, he is notable among

Republicans who are opposed to the Good Friday Agreement and the now predictably defunct Stormont mini parliament. The famous events of Brendan Hughes' life as an Irish Republican activist, hunger striker, and IRA commander in Belfast and within the IRA prison command structure are well documented online and in the book 'Voices From the Grave', based on an oral history project. All accounts of Brendan Hughes' life attest to his working-class socialist worldview, intertwined with his dedication as a Provisional IRA leader, who led from the front during military operations.

His home in Divis Tower Block was bugged, not by MI5 (although they undoubtedly had an interest too), but by former comrades in the Provisional IRA, eager to learn details of the recorded interviews that he made for researchers from the Boston oral history project. The taped interviews detailed many of Hughes' actions in his unit of the IRA, from D Company, based in the Lower Falls area of West Belfast. The ultra-sensitive nature of the taped interviews related to the fact that the Provisional IRA's D Company in the early 1970s was under the overall command of the former President of Provisional Sinn Fein, Gerry Adams.

History shows that insurgents armed with conventional weapons (the gun, the bomb, the rocket) can sustain violent campaigns against state militaries over long periods of time. Victory against such insurgents rarely comes from destruction of troops on a battle field or the streets and as they typically blend into the population, the enemy is often more difficult to find than to neutralize. This situation has reoccurred during the Iraq and Afghanistan wars of more recent operations.

Mike Echo patrols from North Howard Street Mill

Great feeling returning from a 'Mike echo' patrol at the North Howard Street Mill Army Barracks after an all-nighter, located close to the centre of the IRA's Falls Road heartland in West Belfast, The Tactical Area of Responsibility that the unit covered was the predominantly the Catholic area of West Belfast running from the Peace line to the south of the Shankhill Road to Twinbrook and Poleglass in the south, and from the Black Mountain in the west to the MI Motorway in the east. Apart from the 2 small Protestant estates of the Highfields and the Orange Suffolk's, the remainder forms the "Republican Heartland". The areas regarded as hard "Green" (Catholic) include the Lower Falls, Beechmont, Distilleries, Ballymurphy, Turf Lodge,

Lenadoon, Poleglass and Twinbrook estates. It is in these areas that several Provisional Irish Republican Army (PIRA) Active Service Units (ASUs) operate. Most people were law-abiding citizens back in 1986, but many are intimidated and therefore give tacit support to the Republican movement.

The Mike echo patrols covered large areas of ground with the added protection of the armoured vehicles, 'Mike Echo' patrols consisted of 2 x RUC Hotspurs and an Marine APV responding to incidents.

Our 'brick' consisting of four Marines, myself joining with quite a reputation as a bad boy following me, so not to let them down on my first 'Mike echo' I turned up absolutely 'shit faced' tumbling into the rear of the APV and straight to sleep, I don't remember much of that night and I'm not proud of my actions but I was not in a good place personally having recently married to a girl in Gateshead, and by getting kicked out of Recce troop I would lose my Para pay which meant less money to send my new bride.

The Mill was a cramped base camp with little in the way of home comforts like a TV! So me taking comfort in the tins of beer seemed to be the only escape especially after six hours on the main gate. Standing there dressed in the heaviest armoured jacket. For years during the troubles in Northern Ireland, protection lagged far behind lethality on sentry and on the streets of West Belfast. The only practical protection from rounds and dangerous flying objects was the steel plates forward and back slipped into the jacket, but weight forced a trade-off between protection and mobility. Adequate protection did render a Royal Marine perfectly immobile while standing duty on the main gate. A compromise of giving the guy on sentry enough steel to stop light shrapnel or ricochets and other flying objects, but not actual fired rounds.

All body armour fails to protect a target from a sufficiently large and powerful round. Generally speaking, a larger bullet transfers more energy to the target. Back in 1986 the military helmets where not rated to stop large-calibre pistol rounds and shrapnel and definitely unable to stop rifle rounds a helmet capable of stopping rifle rounds would be too heavy and uncomfortable.

The full armoured jacket worn by myself and others on the front gate of the Howard mill back in the day may have stopped shrapnel, but most armour protection lacks coverage for the face, arms, legs and below the waist. The concussive force of explosions can also damage unprotected limbs, create traumatic brain injuries and cause internal injuries even behind body armour.

One 'Dit' told by the older sweats in the company at the time was, a guy on main gate sentry wearing the very same jacket we wore with the two steel plates inside the jacket. The shot missed the front plate and went through his body missing his vital organs but the round then hit the steel plate at the back of the jacket were it then ricocheted back inside him hitting the front plate then once again ricocheting back towards his back before exiting through his lower back. The round made a real mess and killed the guy instantly. I still don't know if this story has any truth to it, it may have been a story to scare the young Marines on the main gate sentry.

Divis Flats foot patrol 1986

Our strategy was constant mobile and foot patrols, which allowed Marines to familiarize ourselves with our area and to pick up background information. Priming patrols to look for key elements by using "face books" of insurgent suspects.

A patrol never ended up at the main gate of the base we would get a quick cup of tea, have a cigarette and in a relaxed atmosphere the patrol would be discussed, and every piece of relevant information written down and passed on to the company intelligence section.

This was to be my first time on patrol with X-Coy, talk about baptism of fire we had to patrol the Divis high-rise flats situated in West Belfast. The Divis a focal point for agitation in the lower Falls area and, therefore, provides a rallying point for PIRA.

On patrol I sometimes expected to be the last man in line, and the feeling of being in the sights of a potential sniper preyed on my mind. Rioting was an almost nightly occurrence. Before long, I was depressed and exhausted. The level of hostility came as a shock. Abuse and bottles of urine were hurled at us. I was not fresh-faced Marine raised in Nottingham still It was hard to cope with the constant banging of dustbin lids, whistling and other noises which kept me on my toes, waiting for the next 'contact' of which we had many.

Patrol tactics showed a very rapid evolution in the early stages of the campaign. Initially a typical patrol would be of section strength with Marines moving in single file. It rapidly became apparent that this was vulnerable, particularly in urban areas, to a gunman engaging an individual soldier at short range and making a quick getaway. Terrain screening usually prevented other Marines from returning fire from their own positions. The initial response was 'parallel patrolling' in which two groups would operate along parallel routes (typically streets). This presented uncertainty to the gunman as to the location of the other group and allowed the group not in the initial 'Contact' to react quickly.

PIRA rapidly developed scouting, observation, and early warning techniques, universally known as 'dicking', which limited the effectiveness of parallel patrolling.

The next development was multiple patrolling in which several small teams (typically three or four teams each of four men) would operate on separate but related routes, crossing and re-crossing, doubling back and acting in what appeared to be a highly unpredictable but mutually supporting manner. Such patrolling became common and the 'multiple', a semi-permanent organisation (typically half a troop) became the standard tactical building block within the company. Multiple patrolling rendered dicking difficult. If patrols did not use the same 5 or 3 routes on a regular basis, multiple patrolling was difficult to overcome. Further uncertainty was created in the mind of the terrorist by varying the number of teams in the multiple. The immediate benefit was that few casualties were suffered by the unit. The longer-term benefit was that it tended to deter shooting attacks.

After one patrol had a contact, it was discovered that patrols had used the same route and the same formation at the same time each day for several days. Within the patrol, teams had developed the habit of following each other up the same street in a formation known as 'duck patrol'. This left the rear team vulnerable, and it was a soldier in the rear team who died. The officer in charge of the patrol resigned his commission.

Divis has been a battleground for the British security forces and the Irish Republican Army. Its tenant's association estimates some 33 residents have been killed by police fire, snipers and army rubber bullets in and around the crime-ridden, crumbling slums in the IRA stronghold of West Belfast.

While on foot patrols in the area rioters would entice soldiers to give chase into an arena from which their fighting could be viewed by hundreds of people on the balconies.

initially we used the Armoured Patrol Vehicle (APV) and then the purpose-built 'Snatch'. The AT 105 'Saxon' was procured in the mid-1980s for use both in Northern Ireland and by UK-based NATO reinforcement brigades.3 Armoured vehicles were extremely useful for the rapid movement of troops, typically to deploy or recover patrols or for Quick Reaction Forces. Operating around the fringes of a foot patrol, they added both speed of reaction and a further degree of unpredictability to patrol movements. However, when operating on their own (singly or in pairs with no foot elements) they were vulnerable to attack. PIRA developed at least two improvised anti-vehicle weapons such as the Improvised Anti-Armour Grenade (IAAG) and horizontal projectors which they deployed in some numbers until counters to them were found. IAAGs were often dropped from overhead walkways or roofs. Counters included avoiding such areas with vehicles, deploying top-cover sentries, and covering movement through such areas with foot patrols.

Overlooking the whole complex and the surrounding area of West Belfast was the Divis Tower a 20-story tower block on Divis Street. It was approved for construction by the Northern Ireland Housing Trust and was one of their few properties built in Belfast's inner city. Completed in 1966 by Laing, Divis is 61 metres tall and It has 95 flats within. It is one of three high rises in Belfast that had an army observation post on its roof. The others were located on Broadway Tower and Templar House, in West and North Belfast. Instead of arriving by lift, we accessed the observation point by helicopter, which landed on the roof. The British army also used the top two floors for several decades and they were not accessible to residents.

Divis Flats was a centre of IRA activity, a battleground, and a deadly place for. It was so important to have eyes on Divis Flats which would have allowed to see Who's coming, who's going, who's armed, what apartments do armed men enter, who's running into Divis Flats ahead of pursuing Marines.

Marines in the fixed observation post can't always see everything; supplemental intelligence, on plain questions about the movements and identities of neighbours who serve in a paramilitary organization, informers, was valuable to the Marines patrolling the area.

Each time the OP changed out the same Marines went to the same position and took over the same watches so we could get used to the routines of the day, such as the milk float on its rounds, the dustman calling, the paperboy on his rounds, and the pubs opening and closing. In this way each marine became familiar with the personalities and locality and was able to spot a change of routine when it occurred.

The one thing information and surveillance could not tell you was the unpredictable actions of residents throwing objects from balconies high above the entrance to the quadrant in the centre of the flats, as you run through the tunnel you know or expect see an object falling towards you like a refrigerator! Or as on one of our patrols a resident pouring hot cooking oil from a frying pan down onto my mate, 'eggman' who quick as you like, shot the guy with a rubber bullet from the 'Baton gun' L5A7 Heckler + Koch 37mm riot grenade launcher with battle sights. The rounds were made from Polyurethane polymer with an additive to increase density, were sometimes exchanged by the lads for a 'D' Battery!

The guy fell out of the window and hurtled down three floors and hit the concrete road below with a thump, dead, or at least he looked dead as we moved out of the flats into cover to wait for the police. On foot patrols you expected to be hit with either a round from the garret sniper or bricks from the kids.

Indeed, urban rumour has it, that one brick of four Marines had a fridge dropped from above as they entered the quadrant inside the flats through the tunnel, urban myth maybe.

In 1985 the IRA leadership sent arms buyers to the United States to acquire the most powerful sniper rifle ever built, the Barrett Firearms M82A1 12.7 mm semiautomatic rifle; this was a serious piece of kit. Then the road signs started to show up ‘Sniper at work’ being hit while on patrol occupied the minds of the Marines more now than ever before. Expecting the ‘Crack and thump’ When you hear the supersonic "crack" of the bullet, you start counting and listen for the "bang" from the muzzle. You mentally align the crack you hear over your head to the thump/bang of the muzzle, there by directing you to the source of the shot.

To estimate the range, you start a quick count (5 counts per second), then multiply the count by 100 to get the distance. So "Crack" 1,2,3,4 "Thump" = 400 meters, easy, but in our case the thump was usually the sound of the round hitting your oppo.

10 British soldiers and RUC killed by the sniper in south Armagh, a desperate attempt to track down the IRA team responsible. The unit was known to operate from a "mobile platform" an improvised armoured saloon car with a gun mount in the back, which made it almost undetectable.

After the attacks, which resulted in 11 deaths (including one in Fermanagh), in only 14 or 15 operations, the sniper was driven away leaving no shells or forensic contamination.

It had been known that the IRA was intent on stepping up its sniping activities since the late 1980s - when several Armagh men were arrested by the FBI in Arizona, as they tried to buy a large amount of military equipment, including Barrett "Light Fifty" .50 sniping rifle.

One of these weapons, which has a range of 2,000 meters, was found in the Central Sorting Office in Dublin in 1986, after an attempt to post it in parts to a Dublin address.

Saturday, September 13, 1986, IRA shot, two men driving through the Crossmaglen area after they refused to hand over their van which was required by the IRA for their campaign of terror.

This sniper unit was on the mind of most foot patrol Marines as they ran around the streets of West Belfast on that summer of 1986, including my own. We operated without a round in the chamber when patrolling the streets, this to stop the negligent discharges that had happened in the past. Personally, I had one up the spout, ready to return fire contrary to the instructions on the 'Yellow card'

The rule of 'don't go into derelicts' was strongly reinforced during pre-tour training, and saved lives. Unoccupied house searches were one factor that led to the development of high-risk search techniques. These were conducted by specialist Royal Engineer Search Teams (REST). Another factor was the PIRA habit of booby-trapping Improvised Explosive Devices (IED) and the areas around them, not least in the hope of killing an ATO. Thus, tasking a REST rapidly became part of the normal response to finding a suspect IED.

An array of all-arms search techniques was also developed. It became normal for each company to have a trained search adviser and a search team, and each Unit to have a unit search adviser All-arms search teams had a limited range of skills and equipment but were a useful contribution to the search effort. In general, once they confirmed the presence of a suspect device REST or ATO was called in. All-arms search teams were particularly useful for route clearance operations. In addition, every Marine in the role was trained in low-level 'rummage' searching. Rummage searches resulted in several important finds. They also reduced the number of effective IED attacks on patrols, and further constrained the terrorists' freedom of operation. 'Winthrop' searching, named after the subaltern who invented it, was a particular technique which effectively got into the mind-set of the terrorist hiding the equipment or device. Procedures were developed whereby in some circumstances the Marine making a find would not reveal the fact; the location would be passed confidentially to his CO who would consider whether a covert operation should be mounted.

Security forces do not 'win' insurgency campaigns militarily; they can contain the level of violence and achieve a successful end-state. They can thus reduce a situation to an 'acceptable level of violence' a level at which normal social, political and economic activities can take place without intimidation. What is required is a level which the population can live with, and with which local police forces can cope. Security forces should bring the level of violence down to the point at which dissidents believe they will not win through a primarily violent strategy and at which a political process can proceed without significant intimidation.

The importance of developing first rate intelligence structures processes and capabilities, so that military operations may be intelligence-led and non-military initiatives properly planned and directed. Effectiveness will be judged by what can be gathered, and by how well the product is shared and used.

It was often said that the British did not understand Ireland. Personally, this reflected my ignorance and an unwillingness to try to understand. For the many who did attempt to understand the roots of the Troubles any number of perceptive books were available. With hindsight what those books could not easily convey, nor the British easily understand, were the deep-seated beliefs, myths and feelings held by the local population. In some cases, the perceived grievances were centuries old. Selectively taught history and the use of events provided rallying cries and strong motivators. Such cultural issues tend to be unspoken and even subconscious. They are inherently difficult to comprehend. In the absence of such deep understanding the British tended to underestimate the differences between the Irish and themselves.

Not resting on our laurels

During the Second World War, a small party of Royal Marines were first ashore at Namsos in April 1940, seizing the approaches to the Norwegian town preparatory to a landing by the British Army two days later. The Royal Marines formed the Royal Marine Division as an amphibiously trained division, parts of which served at Dakar and in the capture of Madagascar. In addition, the Royal Marines formed Mobile Naval Base Defence Organizations (MNBDOs) like the US Marine Corps Defence Battalions. One of these took part in the defence of Crete. Royal Marines also served in Malaya and in Singapore, where due to losses they were joined with remnants of the 2nd Battalion, Argyll, and Sutherland Highlanders to form the "Plymouth Argyll's". The Royal Marines formed one Commando (A Commando) which served at Dieppe. One month after Dieppe, most of the 11th Royal Marine Battalion was killed or captured in an amphibious landing at Tobruk in Operation Daffodil; again the Marines were involved with the Argyll and Sutherland Highlanders this time the 1st Battalion. In 1943 the Infantry Battalions of the Royal Marine Division were re-organized as Commandos, joining the Army Commandos. The Division command structure became a Special Service Brigade command. The support troops became landing craft crew.

A total of four Special Service, later Commando, and Brigades were raised during the war, and Royal Marines were represented in all of them. A total of nine RM Commandos were raised during the war, numbered from 40 to 48.

1 Commando Brigade had just one RM Battalion, No 45 Commando. 2 Commando Brigade had two RM battalions, No's 40 and 43 Commandos. 3 Commando Brigade also had two, No's 42 and 44 Commandos. 4 Commando Brigade was entirely Royal Marine after March 1944, comprising No's 41, 46, 47 and 48 Commandos.

1 Commando Brigade took part in the assaults on Sicily and Normandy,

campaigns in the Rhineland and crossing the Rhine. 2 Commando Brigade was involved in the Salerno landings, Anzio, Comacchio, and operations in the Argenta Gap. 3 Commando Brigade served in Sicily and Burma. 4 Commando Brigade served in Normandy and in the Battle of the Scheldt on the island of Walcheren during the clearing of Antwerp.

In January 1945, two further RM Brigades were formed, 116th Brigade and 117th Brigade. Both were conventional Infantry, rather than in the Commando role. 116th Brigade saw some action in the Netherlands, but 117th Brigade was hardly used operationally. In addition, one Landing Craft Assault (LCA) unit was stationed in Australia late in the war as a training unit.

Marines involved in operation Sea lion: During the Second World War the Irish

Prime Minister Eamon de Valera made his policy clear: the Republic of Ireland would remain strictly neutral during World War II. In June 1940, London even offered to support the principle of reuniting British-ruled Northern Ireland with the South if only Ireland, in exchange, joined the beleaguered British Empire in its conflict with the Axis powers.

But de Valera ultimately refused, distrustful that the government of Northern Ireland in Stormont would cooperate in realizing his long-cherished goal.

Indeed, most of the Irish Republic's leadership had fought the British in the Irish War of Independence two decades earlier. The Republic's small army only 8,000 personnel at the outset of hostilities was even told to prepare for possible British invasion this threat was not entirely hypothetical, as some British commentators did suggest that the UK should consider taking back by force three strategically valuable deep-water treaty ports transferred to Irish control in 1938.

In practice, though, Dublin supported the British war effort in various subtle ways such as by opening a corridor through Irish airspace through maritime patrol planes could fly to hunt German U-Boats. Furthermore, thousands of Irish citizens served in the British armed forces during World War II.

Nonetheless, news of British-Irish tensions reached Hitler in December 1940, inspiring him to suggest that the Wehrmacht should be ready to send troops to the island should Dublin request aid from Berlin—and supply Ireland with British weapons captured during the Battle of France.

German intelligence even schemed to land agents and supplies by seaplane in Ireland—Operation Whale and Sea Eagle—should British troops in Northern Ireland invade the Republic. The Wehrmacht had already begun planning Case Green: an unprovoked invasion of the Irish Republic, to occur in tandem with Operation Sea Lion, the planned amphibious invasion of Great Britain. The German military had never believed that protestations of neutrality should get in the way of exploiting a convenient invasion route. In Ireland, they saw a natural base from which short-range fighters could be more effectively deployed to scour the Royal Air Force from the skies.

Furthermore, a battle for the island would pin down British troops in Northern Ireland, and even deny the island as a last redoubt should Sea Lion succeed in seizing Great Britain, never happened in the end, Hitler ended up going into Russia!

In 1946 the Army Commandos were disbanded, leaving the Royal Marines to continue the Commando role.

Only one Marine was awarded a Victoria Cross in the Second World War, for action at Lake Comacchio in Italy. So far that is the last awarded to a Royal Marine.

Royal Marines were involved in the Korean War. 41 (Independent) Commando was reformed in 1950 and was originally envisaged as a raiding force for use against North Korea. It performed this role in partnership with the US Navy until after the landing of United States Army X Corps at Wonsan. It then joined the 1st Marine Division at Koto-Ri. As Task Force Drysdale with Lt. Col. D.B. Drysdale RM in command, 41 Commando, a USMC company, a US Army company and part of the divisional train fought their way from Koto-Ri to Hagaru after the Chinese had blocked the road to the North. It then took part in the famous withdrawal from Chosin Reservoir. After that, a small amount of raiding followed, before the Marines were withdrawn from the conflict in 1951. It received the US Presidential Unit Citation after the USMC got the regulations modified to allow foreign units to receive the award.

After playing a part in the long-running Malayan Emergency, the next action came in 1956, during the Suez Crisis. Headquarters 3 Commando Brigade and No's 40, 42 and 45 Commandos took part in the operation. It marked the first time that a helicopter assault was used operationally to land troops in an amphibious attack. British and French forces defeated the Egyptians, but after pressure from the United States, and French domestic pressure, they backed down.

Further action in the Far East was seen during the Konfrontasi. No's 40 and 42 Commando went to Borneo at various times to help keep Indonesian forces from causing trouble in border areas. The most high-profile incident of the campaign was a company strength amphibious assault by Lima Company of 42 Commando at the town of Limbang to rescue hostages.

The Falklands war was the next big battle the Royal Marines would fight. Prior to the war, 3 Commando Brigade had just completed arctic training in Norway; hence they were well prepared for the atrocious weather and cold temperatures of the Falklands. The British military didn't boast much after the Falklands. After 10 weeks fighting it was all over, unlike the next two campaigns involving the Corps. Having left the corps in 1989 and becoming a deep sea diver I remember being on the seabed working on a leaking oil-line when the Diving Supervisor told me over the comms, that Iraq had just invaded Kuwait, “where is that”? I replied, he told me 30 miles away!. Just great I thought, I’m in another country that’s been invaded. The year was 1991.

The Royal Marines were involved in the Gulf war in 1991, when they protected Kurdish refugees from Iraqi persecution during Operation Safe Haven. In 1994, a commando unit flew to Kuwait following further threats by Iraq.

The operations since I left the corps are the gulf war in 1991 and in 2000,42 commando deployed to Sierra Leone. Headquarters, 3 commando Brigade and 45 commando to Kosovo. Then in 2002, SBS first Allied troops to land in Afghanistan, and seize landing zone for US Special Forces. Four five commando operations started in Afghanistan. Forty commando deploy to Afghanistan in Special Forces Support role. While Four two commando operated in Northern Ireland. In 2003 Op Telic began with the invasion of Iraq. 3 Commando Brigade amphibious ops and advance to Basra. In 2004,40 commando operational tour in Iraq. Then in 2006 ,3 Commando Brigade (less 40 Commando) Op HERRICK (5) in Helmand Afghanistan. Followed in 2007 by 40 Commando Op HERRICK (7) ,Afghanistan. RM Armoured Support Group (Vikings) in support of army units in Afghanistan. The following year 2008 , 3 Commando Brigade (less 40 Commando) Op HERRICK 9 Afghanistan. In 2010 it was again 40 Commando Op HERRICK 12 Afghanistan. Finally in 2011, 3 Commando Brigade (less 40 Commando) on Op HERRICK (14), Afghanistan.

Royal Marines started on Operation Telic on the 20th March 2003, 40 and 42 Commando moved into Southern

Iraq to secure the oil fields and prevent Saddam from setting them on fire, as he did when withdrawing from Kuwait in 1991. 40 Cdo were helicoptered onto the Al Faw Peninsula in order to secure the oil infrastructure and sweep the area clear of enemy forces. US Navy SEALs worked closely with 40 Cdo in securing a key oil facility.

Later on in 2007 when in Helmand province, Afghanistan, with responsibility and command of the Sangin area of operations, 40 Commando took control. The Commandos will be based here in FOBs and Patrol Bases for the 6 months where they will continue to provide security to the region, mentor the Afghan National Police, partner the Afghan National Army and enable the continuation of reconstruction projects in the area.

The Royal Marines went into action in the mountains of Afghanistan in their first major combat role since the Falklands conflict 20 years before in 1982 In 2012, 45 Commando who took part in the offensive against remaining Taliban and al-Qaida forces in a high mountain valley in the east of the country. The Marines confirmed today that the troops were deployed in combat. From the Bagram air base, near the capital, Kabul, 3 Commando Brigade are operating in the mountains of Afghanistan with coalition partners. The operation is to be targeted on a former Taliban and al-Qaida stronghold.

The Arbroath-based 45 Commando unit, which focuses on mountain- and cold-weather warfare, is part of 3 Commando Brigade, elements of which arrived in Afghanistan several weeks ago. 45 were supported by artillery, engineers and logistics troops as well as troop-carrying Chinook helicopters. 40 Commando, and 45

Commando had training intensively in the Afghan capital, Kabul, for the operation, code-named Jacana. The troops formed Britain's biggest overseas force since the Gulf war.

One of the difficulties that the Royal Marines faced this time is the ability of al- Qaida members to slip across the border to lawless tribal areas of north Pakistan, where they can regroup. Very much like years earlier in Northern Ireland, 45, are now fighting terrorist using counterintelligence methods honed during the troubles. At the same time, Charlie Company, 40 Commando Group, working in conjunction with the Counter-IED Task Force, put in place a cordon around a suspect street to prevent locals from endangering themselves during the clearance and to limit interference from insurgents.

They conduct a routine IED clearance operation. They occupied a rooftop that had good arcs, and remained there while the IED clearance team carries out their Job. Patrols from 40 Commando had identified several IED's in the village and surrounding area over recent weeks .Operations have been mounted to remove the devices but often the Taliban moved them under the cover of darkness to new locations exactly like the IRA.

By using a variety of small arms weapons, which included the recently introduced, 'sharpshooter' rifle The Marines created an observation post so they could speak to civilians to warn them of the danger as well as monitoring possible insurgent positions. A lesson learned from the 1980's during the troubles.

Up on the roof a few lads are covering the operation, with the medic as a CASEVAC [Casualty Evacuation] group, and manning the net. During the course of the operation, which lasted several hours, the Royal Marines and Army bomb disposal experts were fired upon twice, with shots landing a few meters from the bomb disposal expert. Despite this, they moved forward to deal with three suspected devices, which were confirmed along the road and cleared without incident. 40 Commando lost 14 men in 85 days fighting the Taliban in Afghanistan, not expected by the commando standards, losing one man was too many.

A Royal Marine killed in Afghanistan, the fourth commando to die in four days. the marine was on patrol in the Sangin district of Helmand province in southern Afghanistan when he was shot He was on a security patrol, helping to better the lives of ordinary Afghans, when he was killed by small arms fire from insurgent forces. He volunteered and acted as point man for the patrol which his section undertook in Sangin; in my eyes these men, on point, are the bravest of the brave. He was the 300th member of the security services to die. A total of 453 British forces personnel or Ministry of Defence civilians have died while serving in Afghanistan since the start of operations in October 2001.

The following will be remembered, Marine Gary Wright, 45 Commando Royal Marines, Marine Jonathan Wigley, 45 Commando Royal Marines, Marine Richard J Watson, 42 Commando Royal Marines, Marine Thomas Curry, 42 Commando Royal Marines, Lance Corporal Mathew Ford, 45 Commando Royal Marines, Marine Jonathan Holland, 45 Commando Royal Marines, Marine Scott Summers, 42 Commando Royal Marines

Marine Benjamin Reddy, 42 Commando Royal Marines, Royal Marine Corporal Damian Mulvihill,

Marine David 'Dave' Marsh of 40 Commando Royal Marines, Lieutenant John 'JT' Thornton of 40 Commando Royal Marines, Marine Alexander Lucas, 45 Commando Royal Marines, Marine Georgie Sparks, Marine Tony Evans, Corporal Marc Birch, Sergeant John Manuel; Marine Damian Davies, Lance Corporal Steven 'Jamie' Fellows from 45 Commando Royal Marines, Corporal Robert Deering from the Commando Logistic Regiment Royal Marines, Lance Corporal Benjamin Whatley, 42 Commando Royal Marines, Corporal Liam Elms, 45 Commando Royal Marines, Corporal Danny Winter, 45 Commando Royal Marines, Acting Corporal Richard 'Robbo' Robinson, Marine Michael Laski, from 45 Commando Royal Marines,

Christopher Lewis Harrison, of B Company, 40 Commando, Royal Marines, Corporal Stephen Walker, of

A Company, 40 Commando, Royal Marines, Corporal Stephen Curley of 40 Commando Royal Marines, Scott Gregory Taylor, of Alpha Company, 40 Commando Royal Marines, Marine Anthony Dean Hotine, from Alpha Company, 40 Commando Royal Marines; Marine Steven James Birdsall from Bravo Company, 40 Commando Royal Marines,

IEDs will continue to pose a threat throughout the World, that may never go away. They will grow in sophistication and frequency as more enemies of peace realize the potential psychological, social, and political impact a weapon like this provides. No other widely available terror weapon delivers the mass media focus, sheer panic, and strategic influence of the IED.I don't know how true this is, but someone told me that the lads had a one in four chance of losing a limb during a tour of Afghanistan, that might be an urban myth but it certainly gave serving Royal Marines food for thought.

The story ends

My story ends with me walking along the main drag leaving HMS Condor for the last time. Ten years in the Royal Marine family comes to an end in 1989 with me leaving behind some good times along with some very dark times.

Something's will never leave you, no matter what you do, try to push the bad times back into the dark recesses of your mind, while trying to hang on to the good times.

This story is about the troubles in Northern Ireland where many atrocities took place over the years, not only from the communities but also from the security forces and Governments attempting to find a solution.

As the years pass by the world can see that no war or conflict has ever been won when fighting a cause, especially when the beliefs of people are the right to fight and die for their ideals and freedoms.

To beat your enemies, you must understand them intimately and why they would die for their cause, there are lots of things, but willingness to die on the battlefront be it in West Belfast or South Armagh and more recently Afghanistan was both devotion to a tight-knit group of comrades fusion with them and commitment to sacred values. Because most of the military sociology and psychology, at least since World War II, has said that will to fight is based on camaraderie and fighting for your mates.

if people are inspired by beliefs and can inspire others, that group will win out over other groups. And in fact, since World War II, if you look at insurgents and revolutionary groups, they on average beat out standard police and armies with up to 10 times more firepower and manpower, because those police and armies rely on standard material incentives and disincentives like pay, promotion, and punishment. These movements like the IRA rely on commitment.

Human beings are inspired by beliefs and Religious ideologies. This leap of faith seems to inspire great things, and probably is the reason we they able to form large movements people that are willing to sacrifice their family for these things.

It would be useful for our politicians to realize that these people in Northern Ireland Iraq and Afghanistan are not crazy; they're not nihilists or brainwashed. In fact, they argue that we're the nihilists, because we have no moral values anymore.

Without effective cultural understanding the security forces in any theatre cannot conduct a truly effective information campaign and an effective counter insurgency campaign. Many military activities may be flawed because the reaction of population cannot be accurately predicted: there is a need both to gain intelligence and to understand local perceptions. This links to the idea that insurgency feeds off dissatisfaction, and dissatisfaction is a sentiment based on perception. Perception is framed by culture.

During my time working with counterintelligence units in South Armagh I found the job satisfying, thinking I was part of the bigger picture, but on the streets of West Belfast my opinion changed and I thought hear we are acting like paid thugs.

So, as I approach old age reflecting on my actions and the consequences of those actions. I have no regrets by taking part in the history of Northern Ireland and the Falklands war, I sometimes think about the failed operations in Vietnam and Afghanistan, Iraq and Iran and wonder when, as Humans we will understand that no one wins a war.

List of ACRONYMS

AFV: Armoured Fighting Vehicle.

AOR: Area of Responsibility.

APV: Armoured Patrol Vehicle.

ASU: Active Service Unit.

AT: Ammunition Technician.

ATO: Ammunition Technical Officer.

AVRE: Armoured Vehicle Royal Engineers.

BAOR: British Army of the Rhine.

'B' Specials: The Ulster Special Constabulary.

CIRA: Continuity Irish Republican Army.

CIVREP: Civil Representative.

CLF: Commander, Land Forces.

CNR: Combat Net Radio.

CONCO: Continuity Non-Commissioned Officer.

COP: Close Observation Platoon.

CR: Community Relations.

CWIED: Command Wire Improvised Explosive Device.

DAC: District/Divisional Action Committee.

EOD: Explosive Ordnance Disposal.

GOC: General Officer Commanding (all Service personnel in Northern Ireland).

HME: Home Made Explosive.

HSF: (Royal Irish Regiment) Home Service Force.

HUMINT: Human Intelligence.

IAAG: Improvised Anti-Armour Grenade.

IED: Improvised Explosive Device.

INIBA: Improved Northern Ireland Body Armour.

INLA: Irish National Liberation Army.

IRA: Irish Republican Army.

IRSP: Irish Republican Socialist Party.

NICRA: Northern Ireland Civil Rights Association.

NIO: Northern Ireland Office.

NIRTT: Northern Ireland Reinforcement Training Team.

NITAT: Northern Ireland Training Advisory Team.

OA: Operational Analysis.

OIRA: Official Irish Republican Army.

OP: Observation Post.

OPTAG: Operational Training Advisory Group.

PIRA: Provisional Irish Republican Army.

PSNI: Police Service of Northern Ireland.

PVCP: Permanent Vehicle Check Point.

RCIED: Radio Controlled Improvised Explosive Device.

REST: Royal Engineer Search Team.

RIC: Reconnaissance and Intelligence Centre.

RIRA: Real Irish Republican Army.

RUC: Royal Ulster Constabulary.

SB: Special Branch.

SCIAD: Scientific Adviser.

SDLP: Social Democratic and Labour Party.

SLR: Self-Loading Rifle.

SSNI: Secretary of State for Northern Ireland.

SUIT: Sight, Unit, Infantry, TRILUX (ie, 3 times magnification).

TAOR: Tactical Area of Responsibility.

TFATF: Thanks For All The Fish

UDA: Ulster Defence Association.

UDR: Ulster Defence Regiment.

UVF: Ulster Volunteer Force.

UWC: Ulster Workers Council.

VCP: Vehicle Check Point.

VOIED: Victim Operated Improvised Explosive Device.

Printed in Great Britain
by Amazon

63490695R00174